On the road with Hollis
Peavey's Jazz Bandits—1922

THE EDDIE CONDON
SCRAPBOOK OF JAZZ

THE EDDIE CONDON

SCRAPBOOK OF JAZZ

by Eddie Condon and Hank O'Neal

Galahad Books, New York

Contents

Dear Eddie:

I'm glad you telephoned the other night. I had gone to bed tired out with, this one the most — frustrations. No one ever went to pieces from work if the work had any direction. But as usual when that kind of weariness is on, sleep does not come. I was thinking I had all the intricate equipment to build a web, but didn't want the lungs which are the rewards of net builders. Then you phoned and I got to thinking about you and your new book and all the people and noise and experiment that has gone on, experiment by people no more capable of explaining what they are looking for than is a mathematician exploring an unknown but possibly knowable ~~~~~ universe.

I had read a number of the pieces in your new book. And no one has yet put musicians down on paper. The writing about the nervous, restless, exuberant and often angry people who play probably the most universal language of our time is nothing but anecdotes. Pee wee Russel gets a blown ulcer, No one wonders why because Pee wee who can talk circles around anyone living with a clarinet — is almost mute out the power of any other communicating speech. I remember years ago when that book "young man with a horn" came out carrying the message that Bix Beiderbecke was searching for a perfect note, you said in your estimation he was searching for a perfect skinful of gin. I am inclined to agree with your description and yet behind that is something else. Let me try to say clearly what I

3

is not only remarkable — it is almost unique in our time. And I never knew one — a good one that is who stopped trying, who settled back and rested on a satisfactory experiment. I suppose many people know this but do you know anyone who has written it?

The last thing I thought about after your call is the immorality of the language. I've seen 10000 swedes stand in the rain in Stockholm to hear a trio. In Russia I've seen people with no letters of experience try to immitate this inimitable thing by listening to records. And they know when it is good — people who have no right to know — still know — It might be our one real price of creativeness in all the mess of the phoney, the trumped up — the ones sold that passes for creative art in this country. Why, it even withstands the admiring criticism of the priesthood without being warped to precociousness or self adulation.

So Pee wee gets an ulcer, and the biographies are more often than not written on police blotters, and some of them break away to the success of the press agent but always, if they are good or could have been good, with a backward longing look at the purity of the real thing. Any way that's what I was thinking about after you called. You must admit it is a remarkable thing — and it has no historian except you. I'm not speaking of criticism now but of setting down the thing as it is —

Yours
Joe

Foreword by John Steinbeck

Dear Eddie:

I'm glad you telephoned the other night. I had gone to bed tired and with what tires me the most—frustrations. No one ever went to pieces from work if the work had any direction. But as usual when that kind of weariness is on, sleep does not come. I was thinking I had all the intricate equipment to build a web, but didn't want the bugs which are the rewards of net builders. Then you phoned and I got to thinking about you and your new book and all the people and noise and experiment that has gone on, experiment by people no more capable of explaining what they are looking for than is a mathematician exploring an unknown but possibly knowable universe.

I had read a number of the pieces in your new book. And no one has yet put musicians down on paper. The writing about the nervous, restless, exuberant and often angry people who play probably the most universal language of our time is nothing but anecdotes. Pee Wee Russell gets a blown ulcer, no one wonders why because Pee Wee who can talk circles around any one living with a clarinet—is almost without the power of any other communicating speech. I remember years ago when that book *Young Man with a Horn* came out carrying the message that Bix Beiderbecke was searching for a perfect note you said in your estimation he was searching for a perfect skinful of gin; I am inclined to agree with your description and yet behind that is something else. Let me try to say clearly what I am trying to say. I've known musicians—not as you have—but a little. They are the most confused, childish, vicious, vain people I know. On the other hand they are the most generous. Their wills are like those of children. Their cruelties have no more sadistic background than has a small boy when he pulls the wings off flies. Their domestic relations are of mixmaster type. Business confuses them, and so does politics. They almost seem in themselves to live outside ordinary law and common ethics. Now the reason I am saying all of this is that it is also true that I know of no group which has such direction in work. They aim at excellence and apparently at nothing else. They are hard to buy and if bought they either backslide into honesty or lose the respect of their peers. And this is a loss that terrifies them. In any other field of American life, great rewards can be used to cover a loss of honesty, but not with jazz players—a slip is known and recognized instantly. And further, while there may be some jealousies, they do not compare with those in other professions. Let a filthy kid, unknown, unheard of and unbacked sit in—and if he can do it—he is recognized and accepted instantly. Do you know of any other field where this is true? And this curious search for and treasuring of excellence is the one thing that has never been said of them nor written of them. And this whole wordy page is to try to explain what I have always felt—that their inconsistencies may be defense, may be any one of a number of things. This consistency, however, is not only remarkable—it is almost unique in our time. And I never knew one—a good one that is—who stopped trying, who settled back and rested on a satisfactory experiment. I suppose many people know this but do you know anyone who has written it?

The last thing I thought about after your call is the universality of the language. I've seen ten thousand Swedes stand in the rain in Stockholm to hear a trio. In Russia I've seen people with no likeness of experience try to imitate this inimitable thing by listening to records. And they know when it is good—people who have no right to know—still know—It might be our one real price of creativeness in all the mess of the phony, the trumped up— the oversold that passes for creative art in this country. Why, it even withstands the admiring criticism of the priesthood without being worked to preciousness or self-adulation.

So Pee Wee gets an ulcer and the biographies are more often than not written on police blotters and some of them break away to the success of the press agent but always, if they are good or could have been good, with a backward longing look at the purity of the real thing. Anyway that's what I was thinking about after you called. You must admit it is a remarkable thing—and it has no historian except you. I'm not speaking of criticism now but of setting down the thing as it is.

Yours,

John

Introduction

I never knew I had so many photographs. Phyllis saved them all and a couple of years ago when we began sorting them there was never any real plan to publish any of them. We found that some of the photos and clippings were pretty funny and some were downright silly. We thought a few might even be historical. The family, along with Hank O'Neal, picked out the ones that were best and we compiled this book. Some of my friends might not see their faces here, but I am lucky in that I have more friends than photos. Please don't feel offended if you're not in this rogues' gallery; it might be to your advantage.

In a book such as this many people lend their support in a variety of ways. Obviously the major support came from a variety of photographers, largely unknown. We know that many of the photographs in this scrapbook were taken by Charlie Peterson, Skippy Adelman, Gjon Mili, Kathy Gardner and a host of others in 99 per cent of the cases the prints are unmarked. The rest were in the file, taken by Hank O'Neal, various Condons or provided by friends. The various friends were many, including Squirrel Ashcraft, Jeff Atterton, George Avakian, Spencer Clark, Mrs. Stuart Davis, Wild Bill Davison, Frank Driggs, Julius', Max Kaminsky, Jimmy McPartland, Joe Muranyi, Priscilla Rushton, Maxine Sullivan, Dick Wellstood and Mrs. George Wettling. In addition Robert Altshuler and Jerry Valburn provided phonograph records, whose labels we copied. Special thanks are also in order to Annie Laurie Williams who assisted with the John Steinbeck material, Tracy Penton who survived a myriad of design alternations and certainly to Michael Brooks who had the good sense to urge us to get the book started in the first place. Oh yes, there is Les Pockell, our editor, who was forced to tolerate the authors' casual attitudes and impossible schedules. Without Les, there would be no book, and we hope that like the Snopes, he endured. . . .

Oh yes, this book is just for fun. We feel that everything absolutely necessary has been covered adequately and we hope in not too serious a manner. This is mainly a merry visual history of fifty years of American music and we will let you draw your own conclusions.

Back Home Again In Indiana

Goodland, Indiana, 1906. That's where it started sixty-six years ago. In 1947 I put together about fifty pages on all my family-type activities and merry reminiscences of childhood; the kind of things that always turns up in the first part of any biography and they were included in my first book, entitled *We Called It Music*. I don't have any intention of writing all that ancient history down again. If anyone really wants to know about it they can petition Henry Holt to reprint the book or they can go to the local Salvation Army bookstore and search for a copy of the original book.

To set the record straight for those who have neither the time or interest to do either of the above, here are the basic facts. My father ran a saloon in Momence and later in Chicago Heights, Illinois, when Momence went dry. My mother ran the house when he wasn't home. They both had a lot to look after. I was the youngest of nine children, five girls and four boys. I spent most of my time doing what all kids at the time did: chasing dogs, riding horses, going to the swimming hole, and getting into my share of trouble.

My early musical training was mainly sitting around the house listening to my sisters play the piano. I began to play the ukelele when I was about twelve and we had a hot quartet of my dad on violin, my brother Clifford on alto horn, one of my sisters on piano, and a hot ukelele sneaking in whenever possible. By the time I was in high school I was nuts about music and then I got into more than my share of trouble. I left school and went on the road at the age of sixteen. I am still on the road and it's been a joy ride of fifty years. And there are some miles to go.

JOHN CONDON

MARGARET MCGRATH CONDON

FRONT ROW: HELENA, PAT, JOHN, JR., EDDIE, MARTINA

MIDDLE ROW: JOHN, MARGARET

BACK ROW: CLIFFORD, DOT, LUCILLE, GRACE

FAMILY HOME, MOMENCE, ILLINOIS, 1908. EDDIE IN FOREGROUND.

EDDIE IN HIS FIRST PAIR OF LONG
PANTS WITH SISTER DOT

EDDIE, ON RIGHT, WITH HIS DOG DYNA-
MITE, THE DEAN OF THE NEIGHBOR-
HOOD DOGS

DELAYED START

THE SWIMMING HOLE. EDDIE, SECOND FROM

RIGHT, OVERPOWERED.

PHYLLIS SMITH (CONDON)

10 Momence Men of Three Decades Ago Posing for Group 'Shot'

Assembled in front of Condon's Tavern, situated where Stanley's farm store is now located, are 10 men who were active in Momence 35 years ago. The first and last man could not be identified. Others from left to right are Shorty Sherwood, Ralph Day, Will Day, John Mitchell, Bob Haslett, Bud O'Brien, John Condon, owner of the tavern, and George Mitchell. Identity of the small boy in the foreground is also unknown.

The Beginnings and Bix

I went on the road for the first time in the spring of 1922. I couldn't read a note but I could make out song titles and I had my first union card, issued in Waterloo, Iowa, to prove it. I was sixteen and playing with Hollis Peavey's Jazz Bandits. That first summer I covered twelve thousand miles in the backseat of Peavey's car; in the fall of 1971, almost fifty years later, I covered eleven thousand miles with Columbia Artists Management. The roads were a little better in 1971 but I definitely preferred Peavey's car.

By the time I got back to Chicago for a permanent run in 1924 I had spent two seasons with Peavey and had been with Bix Beiderbecke in Syracuse, New York, at the Alhambra Ballroom in between. 1924 was a good year to be in Chicago. I heard Joe Oliver and Louis Armstrong at the Lincoln Gardens and guys like Benny Goodman, Bud Freeman, and Dave Tough were just learning to play their instruments. I got to spend a lot of time with Bix and the migration of musicians to New York had not started. There's always a right time to be in a certain place. This was the right time to be in Chicago.

I stayed in Chicago until the spring of 1928, when I went to New York to see some tall buildings and paved streets. In retrospect it was the right thing to do, although when I left Chicago I had every intention of returning. Bix was one of the first midwestern guys to make an impression on New York and the rest of us arrived about a year later. I found it was just as easy to starve in New York.

Until the fall of 1929 work and record dates were scarce enough, but after the crash employment vanished overnight. Between the crash and 1932 I only made a couple of record dates as a sideman and what little work I had was because I played banjo with the Mound City Blue Blowers, and that group was enough of a novelty that it amused people who still had a dollar to spend in clubs or could afford cocktail parties. I was saved by the Vanderbilts and the Bath Club.

EDDIE CONDON (BANJO), DORIS PEAVEY (ACCORDION), HAROLD CRANFORD (DRUMS), TAL SEXTON (TROMBONE), HOLLIS PEAVEY (CENTER SAXOPHONE)

In 1922 I spent the winter with Hollis Peavey playing the Arcadia Ballroom in St. Paul, Minnesota, and in 1923 the band wintered at the Roseland Ballroom in Winnipeg, Canada. The winter in Canada was one of the best I ever had. The river froze to the bottom and the horse-drawn sleighs and toboggan runs were great. I went on to other adventures after I left Peavey and Peavey went on to become mayor of Huntington Park, California. He might have gone even further if he hadn't played C clarinet.

In 1922 on tour with the Jazz Bandits. We played jazz but we didn't come up the river from New Orleans. Here I am trying to cross the river between Lake Pepin, Wisconsin, and Lake City, Minnesota.

Peavey & His "Jazz Bandits"

A postcard that we sent out to warn everyone we were coming. Someplace, probably in an antique store in Minnesota, there is one that is not torn in half. I don't know how I happened to save this, especially in this condition. I usually don't save anything except vintage upper plates.

JOE HERMAN (PIANO), AL "WOP" WALLER (DRUMS), EDDIE, MOREY POMERANTZ (SAXOPHONE), AL BELLER (VIOLIN)

In 1924 I got a job with Wop Waller's Orchestra at Lake Delavan, Wisconsin, ninety miles north of Chicago. I even sang with the band on rainy days.

DICK SLEVIN, JACK BLAND, EDDIE LANG, RED MCKENZIE

The original Mound City Blue Blowers, after Eddie Lang joined the group. In St. Louis they only used comb, banjo, and kazoo. I once walked seven miles, from Lake Delavan to Lake Geneva, to buy one of their records. I listened to it carefully and seven years later I was a member of the group in New York City.

EDDIE, LAKE DELAVAN, 1925

EDDIE, BUD JACOBSON, MURPHY PODOLSKY

In 1925 I was back at Lake Delavan with Wop Waller and a different cast. That year I wrote my first song, "Laughing at You," and Bud Jacobson put some words to it.

WILD BILL DAVISON AND THE CHUBB-STEINBERG ORCHESTRA AT THE GENNETT STUDIOS IN 1925

The Gennett studios were alongside a railroad track in Richmond, Indiana. Bill never got over the trains.

FRANK TESCHMACHER, JIMMY AND DICK MC PARTLAND, BUD AND
ARNIE FREEMAN, UNIDENTIFIED DOG

*Shades of Austin High. These guys are not the school's bas-
ketball team. With all that hair Bud thought he was certain
to outdo Barrymore and John Gilbert. He's still trying. I made
my first record with three of these guys, Bud, Tesch, and
Jimmy, the year the picture was taken, in 1927. Arnie went
on to be a successful star of stage, screen, TV jingles, and
cruise drummer; Dick played guitar in Chicago until his
death; and the dog became a well-known jazz critic.*

MEZZ MEZZROW, JOSH BILLINGS, FRANK VERNIER,
FRANK TESCHMACHER

Cutting up at White City Amusement Park, Chicago

JESS STACY, GEORGE WETTLING,
FRANK TESCHMACHER (STANDING)

Is everybody happy?

NORMAN SELBY ORCHESTRA

Around Chicago the guys got jobs when and where they could. George Wettling and Jess Stacy didn't come to New York until later and here we see them urging on Norman Selby, his wife, and orchestra. George still had that little drum (directly in back of the alto player's head) when he died.

BESSIE SMITH, 1924

I remember seeing Bessie one night in Chicago in a dump called The Paradise. It was not the first time I saw her but it is the time I remember best. Bix was with me and it was the night he put all his money on the table to keep her singing. We went back every night for a week. Many years later I recreated the scene on one of my TV shows. Bobby Hackett played Bix and Billie Holiday played Bessie. Somebody who didn't know any better played script and it was the weakest part of the effort.

The Wolverines without Bix at the Cinderella Ballroom in New York City in 1924. Jimmy McPartland, who replaced Bix in the band, is holding the cornet Bix gave him. The rest of the band are the guys in striped coats, except Dick Voynow, standing next to the clown in the top row. The floor show cast is spilling all over and one of Bix's early girlfriends, Ann Buckingham, is second from the right in the front row.

GEORGE JOHNSON, MIN LEIBROOK, BOB GILLETTE, DICK VOYNOW,
JIMMY MCPARTLAND, JIMMY HARTWELL

The Wolverines in Florida a few months later. McPartland looks as though he just got off the links. He always liked to knock a ball around, and if possible fix it so that others would have trouble beating him. He once had a match with Bud Freeman and on one green replaced Bud's ball with one that wouldn't roll straight. After Bud hit the ball it not only didn't roll straight but it fell apart. So did Bud. Jimmy won that match.

FRONT ROW: JIMMY MCPARTLAND, VIC BREIDIS, JACK TEAGARDEN
BACK ROW: UNKNOWN, DICK MORGAN, BENNY GOODMAN, FRANK TESCHMACHER,
BUD FREEMAN

Part of the Ben Pollack band with strays

FATS WALLER

(TOP LEFT) ETHEL WATERS

I made my first record in honor of this lady. The day we made Sugar I had just heard her record of same. That's why I didn't sing on the date. She put a lot of songs in business, such as I'm Comin Virginia.

(LEFT) JAMES P. JOHNSON

I got to know James P. in the twenties but never played with him until he made some of my Town Hall concerts and then later some Decca records with one of my bands. He was Fats Waller's idol.

BEE PALMER

I almost got to accompany Bee Palmer. She was instrumental in my bringing Tesch, Sullivan, and Krupa from Chicago in 1928, but when everyone arrived the job we thought we had had fallen through. Bee liked the way we played and got us auditions with other people and we wound up accompanying the dance team of Barbara Bennett and Charles Sabin. We were reviewed as the poorest seven-piece orchestra on earth. We didn't believe our notices. Neither did Bee.

TED LEWIS ORCHESTRA

Ted Lewis played very bad clarinet; he made the clarinet talk and it usually said please put me back in my case. He had good guys in the band, though, and Brunis, Muggsy, and Eddie Lang paid a lot of bills on the salaries he paid. Georg Brunis once remarked that he worked with Lewis for fifteen years, while Lewis was making $10,000 a week, and that all he was worried about was if everybody was happy.

Pat was probably on shore leave when this photo was taken and Mezz was between arrangements. There are not too many pictures of Mezz, other than official ones, but this is a good likeness. I've known Mezz forever and once at the Riverside Towers in New York City, where we were all living at the time, he was talking in his exaggerated down-home style (a style he adopted after the first time he heard Louis Armstrong and it fitted his Southwest Chicago Jewish district like canned ham) to the assembled Chicagoans. We were all pretty down on our luck and here was Mezz moaning in his Dixie dialect when all of a sudden Bud Freeman started wailing and wringing his hand and shouted, "Lawsa massa, I's a weary Jew." Bud's mother was a French Catholic and this act made up for lack of work and Mezz was quiet for at least five minutes.

Some years later in 1946 I bumped into Mezz on the radio show Author Meets Critic. Clifton Fadiman was host, Mezz and his ghost, Bernard Wolfe, were the authors, and Leonard Feather and I were critics. Mezz had just finished his book Really the Blues and at some point I must have made a disparaging remark about the way Mezz arranged music. Mr. Fadiman said that I must be mistaken because a number of famous musicians had told him they were very happy with Mezz's arrangements. He said he even had a telegram from one saying that his arrangements were great and that he should please send more. At this point I immediately deferred to Mezz and the matter was thankfully dropped, right into the lap of the French Line steward who was the main runner. (In Mezz's own way of talking "arrangements" meant marijuana.)

Louis Armstrong and the Luis Russell band advertising some of their instruments

FRONT: MAX KAMINSKY, JOE SULLIVAN, PEE WEE RUSSELL, RED NICHOLS, HERB TAYLOR

BACK: MEZZ MEZZROW, BUD FREEMAN, DAVE TOUGH, EDDIE

Wild Bill Davison found this picture in a junk shop on Eighth Avenue in New York City. It's all that's left of a tour I made with Red Nichols in the spring of 1929. We look like a band of Confederate renegades and the way we acted sometimes proved it. It was a short but hair-raising tour; Bud's all fell out right after this picture was taken. The one thing that stands out in my mind about the tour was that by mutual agreement Red had Pee Wee on an allowance. Pee Wee was always out of cigarette money and Red used to tease him about it, so Pee Wee had to borrow smokes from everybody. Sullivan is pointing at Pee Wee; he probably owed him a pack.

UNKNOWN DRUMMER, EDDIE, UNKNOWN PIANIST, PEE WEE RUSSELL, HERB TAYLOR, RED NICHOLS

My first movie. I never saw it.

(ABOVE LEFT) HOAGY CARMICHAEL

Hoagy, a fellow Hoosier, on an early radio broadcast, singing a song of his, "Little Old Lady."

(ABOVE RIGHT) JIMMY AND TOMMY DORSEY, 1928

What more can be said about these two guys other than that Tommy introduced Gene Krupa, Joe Sullivan, and me to Plunkett's speakeasy on West Fifty-Third Street? Plunkett's was listed in the telephone book as The Trombone Club. I wonder why?

(Left) In 1933 I sailed to Buenos Aires and back and played piano all the way. I'm a good sailor and a bad piano player. I could only play in one key so the entire band played four times a day in the key of F for fourteen thousand miles. The piano was screaming for clemency. Arnie Freeman played drums on the cruise but had to borrow them, and is on the right. Unidentified idiot on left.

The first thing Bix Beiderbecke ever said to me was "hello" in the fall of 1922 in Chicago. He was dead in nine years but played enough for a lifetime. And what he played was better than anything I ever heard. I once described the sound of his horn as being like a girl saying yes. He was the most naturally gifted musician I've ever known. Fifty years later I still remember.

DAVE TOUGH, GEORGE WETTLING WITH WIVES AND GIRLFRIENDS RELAXING IN THE WOODS

THE WOLVERINES, WITH VIC MOORE, GEORGE JOHNSON, JIMMY HARTWELL, DICK VOYNOW, BIX, AL GANDE, MIN LEIBROOK, BOB GILLETTE

PEE WEE RUSSELL, MEZZ MEZZROW, BIX, EDDIE, AND SONNY LEE ON ANOTHER ESCAPADE AT A CHICAGO AMUSEMENT PARK

BIX WITH HOWDY QUICKSELL AND DON MURRAY

BIX WITH THE GENE GOLDKETTE ORCHESTRA, INCLUDING STEVE BROWN,
DON MURRAY, AND SPEIGEL WILCOX

SEATED: SYLVESTER AHOLA, BILL RANK, BIX BEIDERBECKE,
FRANK TRUMBAUER, DON MURRAY, FRANK SIGNORELLI
STANDING: EDDIE LANG, CHAUNCY MOREHOUSE,
ADRIAN ROLLINI, BOBBY DAVIS, JOE VENUTI

Too bad nobody heard this band. It lasted about two weeks and it never recorded; they would have torn a recording studio apart. Joe Venuti looks as though he was just about ready to do something to somebody. I remember one time, a few years later, when he was living at the Plymouth Hotel and Wingy Manone was at the same place, he snuck into Wingy's room and sawed all the fingers off the hand of his wooden arm. He made up for the prank later when he gave Wingy one cuff link for Christmas.

In 1927 I made my first record. There were two sessions and we made four sides. The first two were "Sugar" and "China Boy," and one week later we made "Nobody's Sweetheart" and "Liza." The line-up for the date was Jimmy McPartland, Frank Teschemacher, Bud Freeman, Joe Sullivan, Jim Lanigan, and Gene Krupa. I was the oldest one of the bunch; I had just turned twenty-two and because of this they put my name on the record and since Red McKenzie had promoted the date with Tommy Rockwell at Okeh they put his name on it as well. Later, when Frank Teschemacher became legendary they put his name above everybody's.

This was a pretty significant date. It set a lot of standards that as we grew older we had to live up to and as often as not we did. It was also the first time anyone dared to record a complete set of drums and even though Gene didn't play like Jazz at the Philharmonic it was a good start. We couldn't have made the session without Mezz Mezzrow. He held Gene's tomtoms.

"Liza" may very well be the most significant thing we recorded out of the four. It was the only original; George Rilling and I had put it together for the date. It has words, but thank goodness I didn't try to prove it. Rilling is given composer credit as Ruben on the record, I thought he had changed his name by then. Tesch is responsible for the arrangement, where there is any arrangement at all, particularly the three-horn introduction.

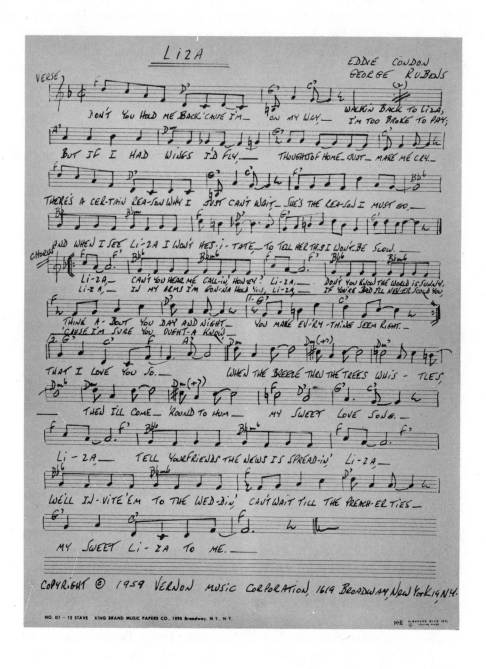

NO. D1 – 12 STAVE   KING BRAND MUSIC PAPERS CO., 1595 Broadway, N.Y., N.Y.

By April 1928 our style of music had started to catch on. At least one person had heard it: Jack Kapp. He ran the part of the Brunswick-Balke-Collender company that made records and he felt some of our stuff should be in the Brunswick catalog. A few of the guys on our first record had gone to New York with Ben Pollack, so we replaced Jim McPartland with Muggsy Spanier and Bud with Mezz Mezzrow. I don't know who held Gene's drums this time. We let Red McKenzie sing on this one, and even though it was not his first effort on records it was his first effort that really got around. He influenced a lot of guys, but he was ahead of his time. He didn't sing through his nose and he didn't sound like a Vienna Boys Choir reject. He just sounded good. The record still holds up today. It isn't hi-fi or any other such nonsense but that's about the only way it is dated. And we were in tune.

The Chicago Rhythm Kings fan club demanded that we cut another side, scarcely a month after we had made the first two. So in May the same bunch of delinquents got together at Brunswick and made a side called "Baby Won't You Please Come Home." The title was prophetic. Everybody was screaming for Red McKenzie to come back from New York once they had heard me sing. I don't know who suggested that I sing, but once the guys at Brunswick had a listen they put the master back in the vault and there it stayed for many years.

In the forties, however, when everyone started demanding Frank Teschemacher records they somehow dug up this old master and issued it. I sang through my nose and couldn't have been in the Hoboken Boys Choir. But when the collectors get loose and want to get things issued, well, you had better watch out. Ordinarily I don't get along with critics very well, but in the program notes to the Tesch album on Brunswick, George Frazier commented, "Aside from Teschemacher's playing, it ("Baby . . .") is notable for one of the worst vocal choruses in the history of recording. It is by Eddie Condon, ordinarily an astute man, and he ends it with a fanciful flourish that is strictly out of a happily vanished era."

This is probably the most obscure record I ever made. I know I made it and I have heard it, but I never saw a copy of the thing when it came out. It was the last record I made in Chicago before I went to New York, in May 1928. Everybody from the Chicago Rhythm Kings date simply walked over to another studio and made this one. We were kings no matter where we turned.

I went to New York in May 1928. I scouted the area and thought this would be a great place to raise a band, so I headed back to Chicago in June and rounded up Gene Krupa, Joe Sullivan, and Frank Teschemacher, and asked them to come to New York. It turned out that it was easier to starve in Chicago. We were all staying in one room at the Cumberland Hotel and looking for any sort of work. We managed to latch onto a record date with Miff Mole and Red Nichols, who had recording contracts under about a dozen different names. We did two tunes, "One Step to Heaven" and "Shimme-Sha-Wabble." "One Step to Heaven" sounds as though it was recorded in a well somewhere. It is a muddle and except for two solo efforts it is barely tolerable. The engineers managed to rearrange the recording balance for the other side and it turned out fairly well. I went on tour with Red a little while later, but this is the only record I made with him. He thought he played like Bix, but the similarity stopped the minute he opened his case.

Three weeks later we were still at the Cumberland and we had not paid them a cent. We had worn out our welcome to the extent that the management had locked up our room and we were in pretty bad shape with the local delicatessens. We owed well over a hundred dollars and there was not any place that would even let us play for free. I went hustling around to the Okeh studios with a Jimmy Noone record I had helped promote on Vocalion and managed to convince Tommy Rockwell that he should record something with a similar sound. I suggested that he use Gene Krupa, Joe Sullivan, Frank Teschemacher, and myself. Rockwell agreed but suggested that one side of the record should have a vocal. I said that I sang on the last record I made in Chicago. I was young, and dumb, and besides, it was my record date. I sang. We made two sides, "Oh Baby" and "Back Home Again in Indiana." Tommy must have made the records out of the goodness of his heart. Okeh never issued them, but they were issued some years later in England. Except for the vocal they are outstanding sides. They represent the only recorded examples of Frank Teschemacher playing without any other horns around him. If Tesch had lived he would probably have been the greatest clarinet player in the world. Of all the people generally associated with me in early Chicago he was the most musically talented, with the exception of Bix, whom he idolized. Tesch was a natural musician. He played all the reeds, arranged well, and even knew how to hold a violin. A remarkable guy.

Trust Eddie Condon to be involved in something different from anybody else. A year after I started doing research at Columbia in 1940 I got a letter from an Australian jazz fan who had found a Parlophone with one side listed as "Indiana" by Eddie "Conlon" and his Orchestra. He was pretty excited and with good cause. There was an alto sax who switched to clarinet and damned if it didn't sound like Tesch. He suspected the pianist might be Joe Sullivan and the drummer sounded like Gene Krupa. There was a banjo who didn't sound like any Conlon ever heard in Australia. And a piping "boy singer," as they used to identify the interruptions on the pop sides of the day.

I asked the Australian collector to send me the record, carefully packed. It was the goods all right, and Eddie checked it out all the way, down to admitting the vocal. You can read the story of how the session came about elsewhere in this book; it's just as Eddie told it to me in 1940—but the ending he gave me then was that they took the one hundred dollars for the date, paid off a ninety-nine dollar hotel bill, and had twenty-five cents apiece left for transparent hamburgers. Later in 1952 I reminded Eddie of the story and he was horrified. "Did I tell you that? Can you see that crowd paying a hotel bill with all that good money, much less splitting the last buck for food?"

But there's more to the lost "Indiana" master. "We made two sides—some Broadway show tune," Eddie said. We turned up a file card at the English Parlophone company, neatly covered with undisturbed dust, giving the title of another side made on that date: "Oh Baby" from the Broadway show *Rain or Shine*. I used both sides in the Tesch album but later when I expanded the album for LP Eddie begged me to cut the "Indiana" vocal. "Tesch boils awfully good behind you," I said. "It's what's up front that counts," Eddie countered. The vocal was clipped and I'm kind of sorry now—I can't find my old 78 version any more and after all these years I can still hear the two splice points on the LP.

—George Avakian

Red McKenzie had come to New York from Chicago to reorganize the Mound City Blue Blowers. He had managed to hire a fiddle, a guitar and Gene Krupa for this date, one of my first in New York City. I didn't even have a banjo for this; I had to borrow one.

I was still boss and didn't know any better. I sang a chorus on "I'm Sorry I Made You Cry" a few months later. The band was called Eddie Condon and His Footwarmers and again it was Okeh who helped with the room rent. The only real difference was that by October it was getting cold and there were more people in the room at night. The "Makin' Frien's" side is sort of a classic. Jack Teagarden sang it and meant it and southmouth Mezzrow can be heard hollering at times in the background. The rest of the band included McPartland and Sullivan, who by that time were standbys; Johnny Powell, a nice guy who couldn't drum much; and Art Miller on bass. I had now sung on three records in a row with mixed results. The first two had not even been issued, and now there was a third. It made it but they held it for a few months before they issued it. Maybe the public wasn't ready. I never sang again on anything that was recorded until 1948, on a TV show marking my first anniversary on NBC-TV.

In 1929 it was easier to hang out in Harlem than midtown after hours and I had some friends at Small's Paradise that made it easier there than most other places. Charlie Johnson had a band there and with any sort of management at all it might have really become something, a rival to Ellington, or anybody else. Charlie's band had made a few records by then but I thought it would be great to take some of the people from his band and team them up with some of my friends. I convinced some guys at Victor to record a small band that I would put together. The guys were Leonard Davis on trumpet, Happy Caldwell on tenor, and George Stafford on drums. They were the people in Charlie's band that I thought were best. Then I rounded up Teagarden, Mezz, and Joe Sullivan. We recorded two songs and they came out pretty good even though somebody was shortsighted enough to call the band Eddie's Hot Shots. It's hard to think back, but I have always wondered why Peck Kelly, the legendary Texas pianist, got composer credits on "Henry Lee." The only thing I can figure is that maybe he put some of the words in Jack's head when they worked together in Texas, because it was a tune we put together the night before.

After the record date was over the people at Victor told me they thought it had been an interesting experiment. This was the first time black and white musicians had ever recorded together. I didn't even think about it beforehand. I guess somebody at Victor did; maybe that was the serious thing.

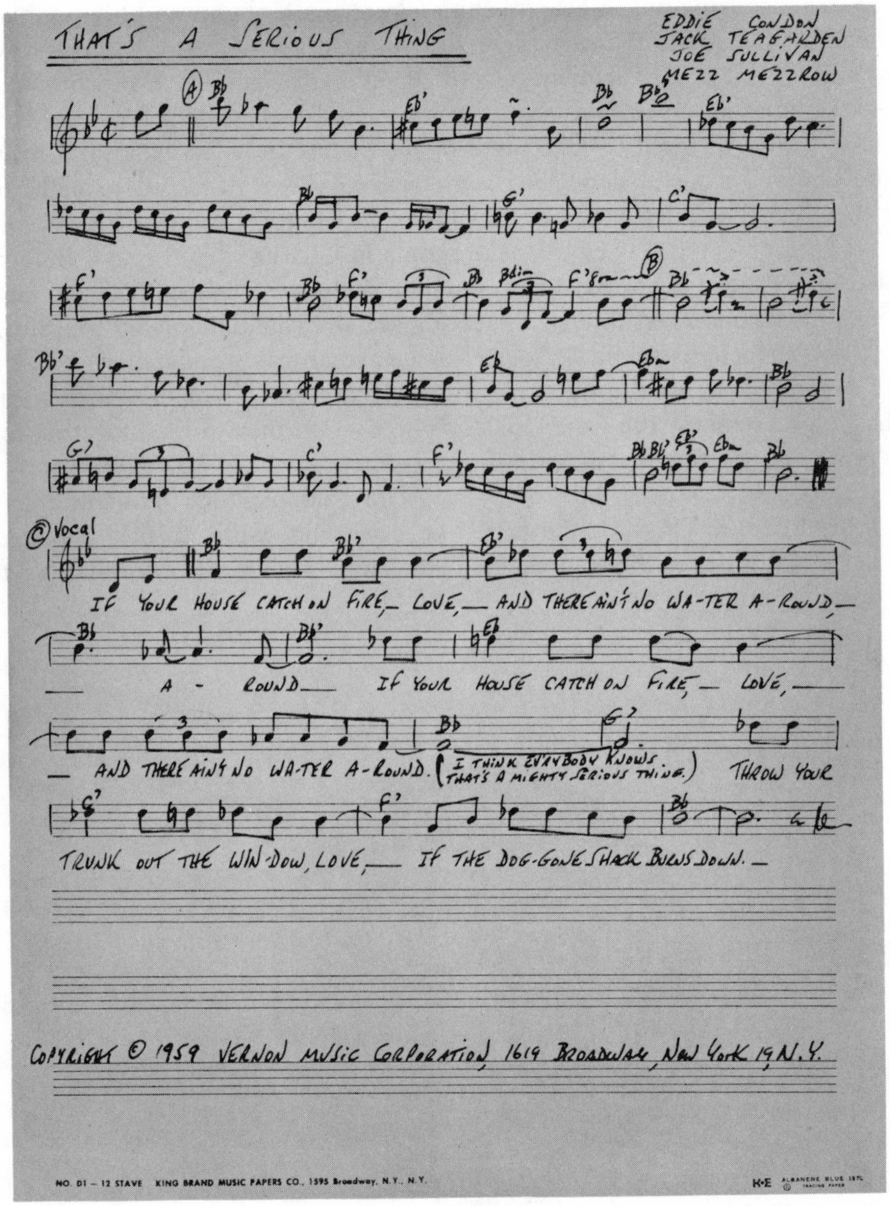
THAT'S A SERIOUS THING
EDDIE CONDON
JACK TEAGARDEN
JOE SULLIVAN
MEZZ MEZZROW
Vocal
IF YOUR HOUSE CATCH ON FIRE, LOVE, AND THERE AIN'T NO WA-TER A-ROUND,
A-ROUND IF YOUR HOUSE CATCH ON FIRE, LOVE,
AND THERE AIN'T NO WA-TER A-ROUND.
(I THINK EVRYBODY KNOWS THAT'S A MIGHTY SERIOUS THING.)
THROW YOUR TRUNK OUT THE WIN-DOW, LOVE, IF THE DOG-GONE SHACK BURNS DOWN.
COPYRIGHT © 1959 VERNON MUSIC CORPORATION, 1619 BROADWAY, NEW YORK 19, N.Y.
NO. D1 – 12 STAVE KING BRAND MUSIC PAPERS CO., 1595 Broadway, N.Y., N.Y.

I first met Fats Waller in 1929, trying to round him up for one of his Victor record dates. I found him at Connie's Inn and the next thing I knew it was one day later and I was waking up after having slept the whole night through on wall cushions at the place. We managed to make the records that day with a bunch of guys I never saw before or since. We were the ones that were in bad shape after having slept on cushions all night long but that's the date the guys at Victor unknowingly reversed the titles on: "Harlem Fuss" is still called "Minor Drag" and vice versa.

After the Hot Shots date we decided to break the color bar at Okeh. In March 1929 I told Tommy Rockwell that he should record Louis Armstrong while he was in New York. Louis was just going to be around for a few days, he was playing a one-nighter in Harlem. Tommy hesitated about my idea of a mixed date but in the end he didn't want to be outdone by Victor. It turned out to be Louis's first date under his own name in New York and four sides were recorded. One was with a small band but I got to play on two of the sides made with the big band from the Savoy Ballroom that made "Mahogany Hall Stomp" and "I Can't Give You Anything But Love." I didn't get to play very much though. Lonnie Johnson was in charge of the guitars and my banjo.

The expanded Blue Blowers, and the first time I had made a record with Coleman Hawkins, Glenn Miller, and Pee Wee. In fact, it was the only time I ever recorded with Glenn or Hawkins. We named the first tune after Pee Wee's then current flame, Lola; it was just a simple tune some of us had put together the night before. "One Hour" was really James P. Johnson's "If I Could Be With You One Hour Tonight." The composer credits on the record are sort of confusing; Gene and Red weren't writing many things at the time. Glenn got a real chance to play on "Hello Lola" and this was the first time Hawkins got to play in a small band like this.

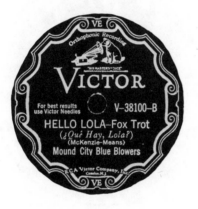

Nick's

I was in and out of Nick's for over a period of eight years with various groups. I moved to Greenwich Village in 1937 to be close to the bandstand when I opened with Bobby Hackett. Nick loved to play the piano. Too bad he couldn't. He had an anvil touch. He had three uprights on the floor and a grand on the stand. The stand was elevated about three feet. When Fats Waller was at the Greenwich Village Inn as the main attraction in the floor show he frequently dropped by Nick's during his long intermissions. One night Fats came by and as the band was playing he sat in at one of the uprights. After playing a few bars on the first one he switched to the second and then to the third. By that time that band set terminated. After a short intermission Fats decided to play the grand on the stand. We played a few bars and Fats leaned over and asked me, with his customary innocent look, "Does Nick make his own pianos?"

Behind the bandstand there was considerable space used as a storeroom for liquor, the inside of which very few people saw. Liquor (especially scotch) at that time was hard to get even though it was legal. Nick, knowing Fats's capacity, thought he would show the well-barricaded interior to him. The liquor was neatly racked, ceiling high. Fats looked around and said, "I'll tell you what you do; put me and a piano in here and lock the door!"

NICK'S IN GREENWICH VILLAGE

OPENING NIGHT AT NICK'S. A GROUP PORTRAIT OF THE TWO BANDS THAT
ALTERNATED, BOBBY HACKETT AND SHARKEY BONANO.

GEORG BRUNIS, BOBBY HACKETT, JOHNNY BLOWERS, CLYDE NEWCOMB,
PEE WEE RUSSELL, EDDIE

ONE OF THE FEW TIMES THERE WAS EVER A VOCALIST AT NICK'S. PROBABLY
LINDA KEENE, WHO OFTEN SANG WITH BOBBY HACKETT'S BAND.

ANOTHER VIEW OF THE BAND

PEE WEE, GEORGE WETTLING, MAX KAMINSKY

This may have been one of the times I was fired.

CLIFF JACKSON, FREQUENT INTERMISSION PIANIST

NICK'S, at Seventh Avenue and 10 Street in Greenwich Village, is still smoky, crowded and wonderful. The band, which is led by valve trombonist Brad Gowans, has Pee Wee Russell, playing better than he has in ages, on clarinet; Eddie Condon on guitar, Chelsea Quealey on trumpet, Danny Alvin on drums and Dick Carey on piano. Night in night out, it seems to me the most satisfying band working in Manhattan at the moment. Beer costs 20c, the musicians fear nobody (especially Nick) and the whole atmosphere is conducive to the right jazz.

NICK AND CLIFF JACKSON AT THE PIANOS. BRAD GOWANS, EDDIE,
DANNY ALVIN, CHELSEA QUEALEY, PEE WEE, UNKNOWN BASS.

THE SUMMA CUM LAUDE ORCHESTRA WITH DAVE BOWMAN, EDDIE,
PEE WEE, STAN KING, MAX KAMINSKY, CLYDE NEWCOMB, BUD FREE-
MAN, AND BRAD GOWANS

*This was one of the best bands that ever played in Nick's or any-
where else. We were cooperative and sometimes even rehearsed.
Phyllis Smith named the band and though nobody could pronounce
our name and even when they did it came out Over Come Loaded
or worse we played just like the name implied.*

GET OUT — YOU'RE FIRED

NICK

P.S. — I COULDN'T SAY THIS TO YOUR FACE — MY BREATH HAS BEEN TOO LOATHSOME THE PAST WEEK.

John DeVries in disguise

Outside Nick's—1939

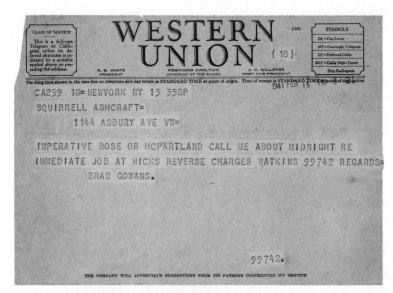

Fired again

EDDIE AND JOHNNY O'CONNOR

Johnny was my manager until the day he died. He did his job. He was telling me to stay out of Nick's, and he introduced me to Pete Pesci who was managing Julius's, where this picture was taken.

GEORG BRUNIS, PEE WEE, WILD BILL, DANNY ALVIN

The Peerless Quartet alive and well at Nick's. Georg is standing on Pee Wee's toe.

BOBBY HACKETT, VERNON BROWN, EDDIE

Barney's was up Seventh Avenue from Nick's. They didn't always sell those modern Italian suits.

Nick Rongetti Dies; Pianist Ran Night Club

His Jam Sessions at Nick's Included Eddie Condon and Fats Waller in Group

Nick Rongetti, forty-eight, jazz pianist and proprietor of Nick's, night club at Seventh Avenue and Tenth Street, died yesterday at St. Vincent's Hospital, Seventh Avenue and Eleventh Street. He lived at 99 West Twelfth Street.

In jam sessions at Nick's he put into practice his theory that jazz musicians should be free to "play as they please." There is no sheet music on the bandstand in these sessions, and musicians smoke, talk and stroll about informally while not actually playing.

Eddie Condon, electric guitarist, who has put on several such concerts at Town Hall, helped to organize the sessions and often took part in them. Another who frequently sat in was the late Fats Waller, pianist.

Mr. Rongetti attended Georgetown University, Washington, and was graduated in 1927 from Fordham University School of Law. He then studied medicine for a year at Long Island University, Brooklyn.

He gave up his medical training to become a piano player at Greenwich Village night clubs, and soon afterward opened his first place, Nick's Tavern, at 140 Seventh Avenue. He moved to his present place ten years ago.

Surviving are his wife, Mrs. Grace Rodgers Rongetti; a son, Jay, six; a daughter, Judy, eight, and a brother, Dr. Joseph R. Rongetti, assistant visiting ear, nose and throat specialist at St. Vincent's Hospital.

I never played electric guitar, even for Nick.

The only records I made in 1932 were a series for ARC that was loosely called the Rhythmakers, even though they were issued under Billy Banks's and Jack Bland's names. I hired the bands for all the dates and each time called Red Allen, Pee Wee Russell, Jack Bland, and Zutty Singleton. We filled in the dates with Fats Waller, Joe Sullivan, Tommy Dorsey, Pops Foster and a few other guys. The records were uniformly very good and still sound good even though they are forty years old.

The first date under my own name in four years. I figured if they were brave enough to put my name on a record things might be looking up. I was wrong. It took five years for it to get on one again.

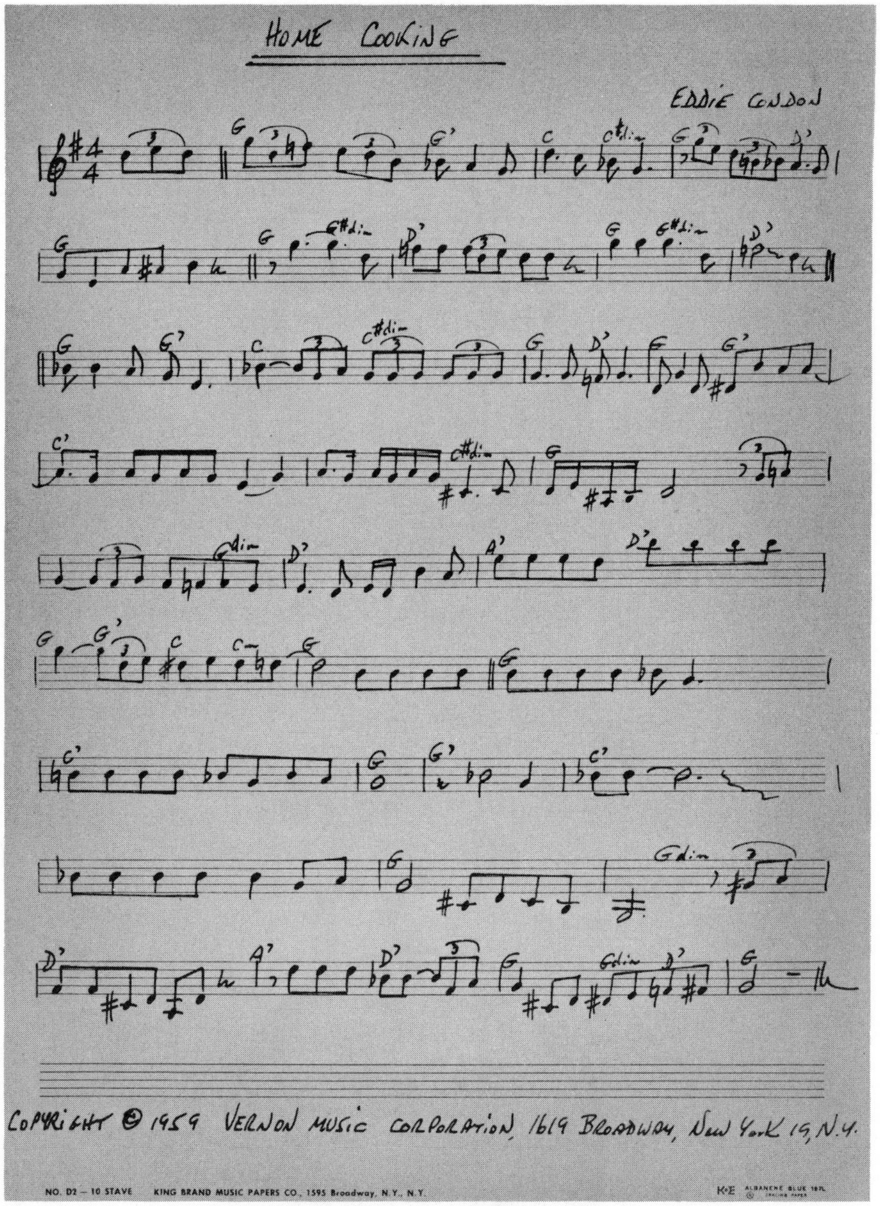
HOME COOKING
EDDIE CONDON
COPYRIGHT © 1959 VERNON MUSIC CORPORATION, 1619 BROADWAY, NEW YORK 19, N.Y.
NO. D2 — 10 STAVE KING BRAND MUSIC PAPERS CO., 1595 Broadway, N.Y., N.Y.

Bud had a long time between runs with records too. He made this in 1935 and had had seven dry years as a leader on records. Tillie ran a rib joint in Harlem. We used the proceeds from the record to buy a meal there.

Red still kept getting record dates even though he didn't have much of a following. He was too good for that. I'm glad that he asked me to play along.

A record by Bunny Berigan. I am not on "I Can't Get Started" even though the scholars who think they know say I am. I was dying in Polyclinic Hospital on the day it was made but in a small way I helped Bunny get his theme song together by suggesting the chordal changes going into the last chorus. Johnny DeVries is really responsible for Bunny having made the tune in the first place. Johnny heard the song in the 1936 Vernon Duke Show and thought it had little exposure. After insisting for a couple of months that Bunny play the song he went to the publisher himself and got an orchestration of it. He hummed the tune to Joe Bushkin who in turn played it for Bunny. Bunny and "I Can't Get Started" have been inseparable ever since.

One of the Over Come Loaded's better projects: an entire album of tunes Bix had made with the Wolverines. (I had thought of calling it *Sons of Bixes* but I couldn't get away with it.)

After I opened with Bobby's band at Nick's in 1937 Sharkey decided that I could play a little guitar and he used me on some of his dates. Sharkey plays well, but he should have kept his mouth closed, like I eventually learned to do.

After Bobby Hackett took the band into Nick's he signed with Vocalion and made a series of records. He had a good two-year run with that label and I managed to turn up on the first dozen records. On the early recording he used the band as it was at Nick's at the time, including, in this case, the girl singer.

The Park Lane and Ryan's

In the spring of 1938 two of my friends in the advertising business, Ernie Anderson and Paul Smith, who turned out to be my brother-in-law, started thinking up ways to lure some of the guys they worked with to hear some jazz. They came up with the idea of putting on jazz concerts late Friday afternoon in the Madison Avenue area. There weren't many accommodations on the street so they started shopping around for a hotel ballroom to use. Everyone turned them down before we even had a chance to blow a note until finally they made a deal with the Park Lane to rent their unused ballroom. The concerts got off to a good start. For the first concert I rounded up twenty-two guys and things went well for many months. At one concert, however, a senior director of the New York Central, the company that owned the Park Lane, came in for a drink and he couldn't get near the bar. He was not used to such merriment on the staid old Park Lane premises and he was shellshocked. That ended our very successful run at the hotel. We later resumed the series at the Belmont Plaza.

Joe Marsala was master of ceremonies. Here he is conducting. Note that Pee Wee is paying close attention.

ZUTTY SINGLETON, BRAD GOWANS, MORTY STUHL-
MAKER, MARTY MARSALA, EDDIE, BOBBY HACKETT,
PEE WEE RUSSELL, BUD FREEMAN, SIDNEY BECHET,
JOE MARSALA

Same concert, cheering Pee Wee on. Marsala still on mike.

the
friday
club

BY PHYLLIS REAY

TRUE jazz music has a cult of its own. Its followers are as frigid to popular current "arranged" swing as they are to Guy Lombardo, Johannes Brahms. Hard, fast and faithful to the rigid, intellectualized (but hot) style known as "Chicago" or "Dixieland," these musicians and music lovers have still found no prophet to out-trumpet the late Bix Beiderbecke, no leader to out-clarinet the great and simple Teschmaker. Among a small group of living artists, however, the style they look for still exists.

Not in one single band. Not in any band. But in the living styles of a scattered group of musicians (most of them now playing in large commercial bands). These men, with their backgrounds of improvisation, easy knowledge of the great jazz tradition—are now in demand by highly paid organizations, for their spontaneity, solid tempo. They are employed by Whiteman, Dorsey, Shaw, Berigan; some have their own bands.

In the Friday Club cultists and musicians have gotten together. Have done something about preserving the great tradition that Bix and Tesch so far advanced.

Here, such names as Fats Waller, Bud Freeman, Pee Wee Russell, Jimmy Dorsey, Eddie Condon, Artie Shaw, Bobby Hackett, Jess Stacy, Arthur Schutt, George Wettling will come, play, or just attend.

The mid-town office crowds, music lovers—many who work in the busy 40's and 50's—have accepted this idea enthusiastically. Here they start their week-ends. Here the scattered Mid-West boys with their music followers will again pick up, accumulate, add to that strange phenomenal store of blues, jazz, musical ideas—that flashed out so unaccountably during the late '20's.

Here once again can be heard that unmatchable, stomp-down, free-style music which started in Chicago dance-halls; little, cold, one-night-stand towns along Lake Michigan—just ten short years ago.

JOHN DE VRIES AND MILT GABLER WITH WILLIE THE LION SMITH

EDDIE, STERLING BOSE, PEE WEE RUSSELL, WILLIE, ZUTTY SINGLETON
AND BOBBY HACKETT

*Willie is usually thought of as a solo player but he could kick a
band along as well. The only guy here I knew longer than Willie
was Sterling Bose. I first saw him when I was sitting in at the
Midway Gardens in Chicago. He proved he could play there, but
even before that he proved it in St. Louis playing opposite Bix.
He's sitting next to Pee Wee here; he sat opposite him in St. Louis.*

BUD AND SIDNEY BECHET

BUD AND LIPS PAGE

We always had our share of trumpet players. Here are a few views of some of our line-ups.

TWO OF THE SPIRITS OF RHYTHM

ARTHUR SCHUTT

We were lucky to get Arthur Schutt for these concerts. At one time he was making so much money writing arrangements for just about everyone that he could have sponsored the concerts himself. He was a debonair guy; he always wore a flower in his lapel.

EDDIE, ZUTTY, BOBBY HACKETT, MORTY STUHLMAKER, JIMMY DORSEY, PEE WEE

Two of the most peaceful guys in the world on reeds, and one of the few times they ever played together.

AT EASE

BUNNY BERIGAN, RED MC KENZIE, BUD, AND FORREST CRAWFORD

After our difference at the Park Lane we moved over to the Belmont Plaza but the concerts were never the same. The atmosphere was different and we only played a few more Fridays. We still had the great talent but the novelty had worn off. One of the concerts we had Bud and Forrest Crawford in the band and it was the only time I know the two played together. Forrest was a good player who wasn't around very much. He popped in one day in the mid-thirties and then one day he wasn't around any more.

From 1940 through 1945 Milt Gabler ran a series of jam sessions at Jimmy Ryan's. The sessions were on Sunday afternoon from early fall until late in the spring. They might have run year-round if there had been air conditioning. When things got going almost anything could happen and it looks as though almost everything is in this picture.

This is one of the few pictures of Jack Bland, directly over my head. When Eddie Lang was added to the Mound City Blue Blowers he only had to learn three songs. By this time Jack probably knew half a dozen; he looks like he is trying hard though. He finally migrated to California after he helped with my Town Hall series and wound up driving a cab and working for a messenger service. He died there.

Happy Caldwell is on tenor. He was on some of the Rhythmakers records and still lives in Harlem. Other than myself he's the only guy in the front row still alive and he was middle-aged then. The back row doesn't make out much better.

SIDNEY BECHET AND HOT LIPS PAGE

*This was about the time Bechet was in the clothing business.
Except for jam sessions like these there was not much work.
Both guys are trying here.*

PEE WEE, BRAD, BOBBY HACKETT, JOE SULLIVAN, MARTY MARSALA

JOE SULLIVAN

The kitchen was right behind the bandstand at Ryan's. Joe doesn't seem to mind here. At some places on Fifty-Second Street it was hard to tell the difference between the kitchen and the washroom and I know of one wash-room attendant who quit because of the odor from the kitchen.

ZUTTY

EDDIE, GEORGE WETTLING, SANDY WILLIAMS, BOBBY HACKETT,
MAX KAMINSKY, PEE WEE RUSSELL, JOE SULLIVAN, UNKNOWN
BASSIST, BENNY MORTON

TRIO

More Jam Sessions

You often have the best times when you get a bunch of guys together who don't play together regularly. As often as not in the thirties and into the forties they were not playing at all so jam sessions provided a remedy for both these problems. The best ones were often in the homes of musicians or their friends; there have been a few in my living room where everyone was unsorted and disorganized. Sometimes the music turns out bad, sometimes awful, but if the mood is good and there is enough to drink only the good memories last.

TWO SIDNEYS, BECHET AND CATLETT

FRONT: TOMMY DORSEY, LOUIS ARMSTRONG, GEORGE WETTLING
BACK: BUD FREEMAN, POPS FOSTER, EDDIE

Backstage at the Paramount Theater. The guys just dropped by with their instruments and Charlie Peterson took the pictures. One of the series ran in Life in an article that Alexander King put together.

JOE SULLIVAN, PEE WEE RUSSELL, ZUTTY SINGLETON, BOBBY HACKETT, BRAD GOWANS, EDDIE, MAX KAMINSKY

Three views of our concert at the Walt Whitman Progressive School. A twist of fate: Thirty years later my daughter Maggie worked in the same building with Bert Stern, the photographer.

ART HODES, ROD CLESS, GEORG BRUNIS

As for the stack of music, Georg can't read it. He can barely lift it.

CHICK WEBB, DUKE ELLINGTON, AND ARTIE SHAW

Chick was one of Gene Krupa's favorite drummers.

Same jam session with Joe and Marty Marsala, George Wettling and Joe Bushkin

A gathering at Burris Jenkins' (famous cartoonist for the old New York Journal) studio. It was staged by Life magazine. They rounded up part of the Ellington band and a lot of guys who were talented and available. The music was exciting, except for one snag; Ellington had part of his payroll (cash) in his suitcoat pocket. It was a hot night and he removed his coat, which he hung on the back of the chair. When the party ended, hours later, Ellington had a coat but no payroll.

DAVE TOUGH, EDDIE, COZY COLE, BILLY TAYLOR

EDDIE, BRAD GOWANS, JUAN TIZOL

ENSEMBLE WITH DUKE ELLINGTON LEADING ON GUITAR

HIGGY, BRAD, JUAN, LIPS, REX, AND MAX WITH DUKE AND EDDIE

BILLIE HOLIDAY, MAX KAMINSKY, EDDIE, CLYDE NEWCOMB

BUCK CLAYTON, BUD, DAVE BOWMAN,
GEORGE WETTLING

Misha Reznikoff and some friends at one of his jam sessions

*Lips Page after hours. George Wettling in
background.*

JACK TEAGARDEN

Just Friends

Some people try to categorize everything. Music critics are always trying to categorize jazz as this kind or that kind and they only wind up categorizing themselves. Some pictures fall into place in this scrapbook but many don't. Here are some of my friends, playing and relaxing many years ago. This is the way things looked to me in the thirties and forties. I didn't see myself in the pictures everybody took and this is the way I remember these guys.

GEORGE WETTLING WHILE HE WAS WITH PAUL
WHITEMAN IN 1938

JIMMY MC PARTLAND, JACK TEAGARDEN,
LOUIS ARMSTRONG

BILLIE HOLIDAY AND JIMMY MCPARTLAND

Jimmy's trying to sell Billie one of his albums.

Arthur! No flower?

Wild Bill at the Ken Club, Boston, 1939. I don't know where he stole Brad Gowan's valve trombone.

The whole band a night later with a very young Gene Schroeder and Pee Wee Russell

BOB CASEY, BABY DODDS, FLOYD BEAN, JIMMY NOONE, ROY ELDRIDGE

EARL HINES

After I made my first records for Brunswick in 1928 Red McKenzie and I took Jack Kapp, the head of Brunswick, to the Apex Club, located in the heart of the South Side district. We wanted to sell him on the band there led by Jimmy Noone and featuring Earl Hines. Kapp was impressed and he managed to convince Noone to make a 10:00 A.M. recording date for his subsidiary label, Vocalion. These pictures were taken at least ten years later; Jimmy never left Chicago and never achieved anything like Earl's following.

EDDIE, JOE BUSHKIN, JOE MARSALA, MORTY STUHLMAKER, RED ALLEN

One of the first mixed bands on 52nd Street in 1936

Paul Whiteman kept a few of my pals employed in the thirties. You can see Miff Mole, George Wettling, and Frank Signorelli if you look closely.

Louis Armstrong and Maxine Sullivan dancing at the Cotton Club in the late thirties; I was in the Cotton Club at least once, but not that night. Maxine still looks just as pretty and sings better now than ever.

Stumped again. The Yank Lawson Trio?

GEORGE WETTLING AND BUNNY BERIGAN

These two guys always looked good and played better. At the time this picture was taken George was drumming in Bunny's big band and here they are on the sidewalks of New York. It has to be New York; look at the Nedick's sign in the faded background.

A handsome picture of Billie

Sidney Bechet and Tommy Ladnier at one of the Bluebird sessions organized by Hughes Panassie. I don't know where Hughes is; maybe he was out jumping on a grape. Mezz was also on the date; maybe he was out in the hall picking cotton.

RED ALLEN, PEANUTS HUCKO, ED HALL

A room with three views. A casual session; this is the way Red usually looked.

In December 1936 a gang of American pirates took over the Empress of Britain for a nine-day cruise. I had an eight-piece band made up of Marty and Joe Marsala, Joe Bushkin, Artie Shapiro, Al Seidel, and three guitar players, Paul Smith, Pat Condon, and myself. I conducted and the other two guys played guitar. We stopped at Jamaica, Cuba, and Bermuda, had New Year's Eve at sea, and didn't have to play very much. We scared some of the aristocratic people half to death; they were certain we planned to make them walk the plank. But we usually just ignored them. We were too busy having a good time.

EDDIE, AL SEIDEL, COLIN CAMPBELL, ARTIE SHAPIRO, JOE MARSALA, MARTY MARSALA, JOE BUSHKIN, TAXI DRIVER

It's obvious I don't like rum.

AL SEIDEL, EDDIE, JOE MARSALA, MARTY MARSALA

Two relaxing socialites and unwanted intruder

PAT CONDON AND JOE MARSALA

Empress of Britain *exercises*

Joe Bushkin holding a Paul Smith sketch of a dancer in the floor show

BUNNY BERIGAN WITH TOMMY DORSEY. BUDDY RICH IN BACKGROUND.

BILLY BUTTERFIELD WITH THE BOB CROSBY ORCHESTRA. RAY BAUDUC
ON DRUMS.

EDDIE, JIMMY MC PARTLAND, PEE WEE RUSSELL, JIM LANNIGAN, JOE SULLIVAN

We had all gone out to a Chicago suburb to see Jim Lannigan's trained crow on this summer day in 1942. Some guys marry crows, Lannigan was the only person I knew who kept one as a pet. Jimmy McPartland, who won three letters at Austin High for croquet, had just found a mallet and challenged us all. He probably won; if he had learned to kick the ball quicker he might have made the Olympic team.

This picture was taken on a historic day in my life. After we finished the match, Jim drove us back into Chicago. As we were driving down a street in West Chicago I saw a big schoolhouse. I asked what it was. Lannigan replied that it was Austin High School. Krupa and Sullivan and I were supposed to be part of the "Austin High Gang," a name pinned on us by critics who have to put labels on everything. I couldn't spell Austin High. I'm glad I finally saw it.

The best husband and wife duo in jazz at the time. Lee Wiley and Jess Stacy.

RAY BAUDUC

PHOTOGRAPHER CHARLIE PETERSON, JACK TEAGARDEN, AND
TEACHERS

On that swanky street

Jack Teagarden inside

JAMES P. JOHNSON

AND THE REST OF THE QUARTET: EDDIE, ROD CLESS, AND
GEORGE WETTLING

FRANK SIGNORELLI, PAUL WHITEMAN, HUGHES
PANASSIE, JACK TEAGARDEN, GEORGE WETT-
LING, MEZZ MEZZROW, TOMMY DORSEY

*Too many leaders here. What did they
sound like? What are they doing? Is Mezz
in charge? Hughes thought so, and probably said so in his book on the table.*

Another Freeman convert

(Above) In 1938 we made the first transatlantic radio broadcast of a jazz concert. The broadcast was from the St. Regis Hotel and everyone who could breathe was there. Alistair Cooke was M.C. We played and had a good time. At one point Mezz Mezzrow grabbed the mike and said "Hello England, this is Mezz!" George Avakian was there and here we are pictured on the roof during an intermission. He was the only guy there who didn't play. Some years later I made a gang of records for George when he was at Columbia and I learned some years later that he had talked to Ed Murrow about the St. Regis broadcast. Murrow had handled all the chores for the concert in England and he told George that it was one of the finest broadcasts he had ever worked on.

FLOYD O'BRIEN

MAX KAMINSKY, WILLIE THE LION SMITH, ROD CLESS IN 1944 AT THE PIED PIPER

The Pied Piper was a small club in the Village on Barrow Street that prospered briefly. It looks like W. C. Fields on clarinet.

Milt Gabler's Commodore Music Shop on Forty-Second Street. He made records that were named after the shop. They were all jazz and all good.

The first time I met John Hammond I was with the Mound City Blueblowers at the original Stork Club on West Fifty-Sixth Street. He was fascinated with Joe Sullivan's piano playing. Joe was working with us then. Shortly afterwards he invited us to his home on Fifth Avenue. We expected a drink or two and we were not disappointed: tea and cookies.

FRONT: MAX KAMINSKY, JACK LEONARD,
DAVE TOUGH
BACK: BUD FREEMAN, AXEL STORDAHL

The basketball team from Tommy Dorsey's Orchestra

SPENCER CLARK, JACK PURVIS, GEORGE CARHART

The last time I heard of Jack Purvis he was climbing the Alps in his bare feet.

BOB CROSBY, EDDIE, BOBBY HACKETT, ADRIAN ROLLINI, JACK JENNY

EDDIE, JOE SULLIVAN, JOSEPH SZIGETI, JOE MARSALA

Szigeti is asking Joe and Joe to play the Bartok Contrasts with him. I am considering conducting if Benny Goodman wouldn't mind.

Dave Tough and Cozy Cole at cartoonist Burris Jenkins' studio. It was hot that night and so was the hooch.

A *remarkable shot of* Georg Brunis

George Wettling *practicing his roll*

BUD FREEMAN AT THE JOE HELBOCK
CONCERT, 1936

Lee Wiley making Liberty Music Shop's first record, an Ernie Anderson promotion. The best thing that ever happened to Liberty Music Shop.

Three views of my former room-mate, Max Kaminsky

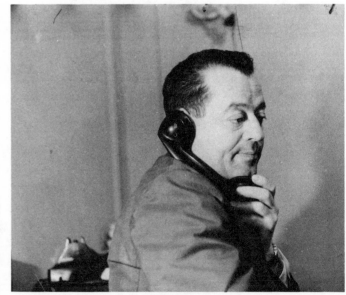

LOUIS

BOBBY HACKETT IN THE VILLAGE A
FEW YEARS AGO

CHARLIE TEAGARDEN, JIMMY MCPARTLAND,
JIMMY DORSEY

EDDIE, JESS STACY, ERNIE ANDERSON, LEE WILEY, AND JOE CLOSE ON LUDWIG BEMELMAN'S SPECIALLY PAINTED PIANO

LOUIS, ZUTTY, AND CHARLIE PETERSON

Mezz has been a Paris resident for some years.

ROD CLESS, JOE THOMAS, JAMES P. JOHNSON

STELLA BROOKS, JOE SULLIVAN, RED MCKENZIE

TEDDY WILSON AND DON REDMAN, GEORGE IRISH, AL HALL

KAISER MARSHALL, ROD CLESS, WILD BILL, SANDY WILLIAMS, JAMES P. JOHNSON

Coleman Hawkins and some of my pals

CLIFF JACKSON

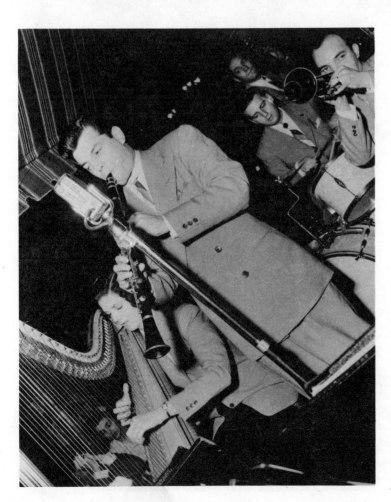

JOE, MARTY, AND ADELE MARSALA AT THE HICKORY HOUSE

Bing and Bud jam in our living room

EDDIE CONDON AND JOHNNY MERCER

Recently I had occasion to inquire of a little boy what he wanted to be when he grew up. Without breaking the Chicago-style beat of his bubble gum he replied, "Eddie Condon." Conference had been fogging my vision a bit of late. It was clear that the little boy had his hip boots well clasped up to his navel. This was the jolt I needed. I played an old Punch Miller record with a George Wettling backing I had recently dubbed in, added a configuration to my current painting, "The Mellow Pad," and forgot all about Sir Alexander Cadogan and Gromyko. For a brief moment I thought I was Eddie Condon too, but that passed.

Stuart Davis—1947

George Wettling learned to paint at our apartment in 1943. We were moving and to get back at a pesty super we decided to have a wall-painting party. George was our most enthusiastic painter. When he ran out of walls at our apartment he left immediately for Stuart Davis's where he found lessons and encouragement. His first painting was of our daughter Maggie. She forbids reproduction.

My fiftieth birthday present from George. He told me to look out for the black bottle. I still am.

George Wettling *painting with Max, Pee Wee, and Freddie Ohms in the early fifties.*

Baby Dodds. Baby gave George one of his cymbals. George used it right up to his last run at Bill's Gay Nineties.

HE SAYS HE LEADS
A BAND —

JAMES MONTGOMERY FLAGG

Chicago

The mass migration of musicians from Chicago to New York was complete by 1930. After 1930 the jazz in Chicago was an underground thing, except on Monday nights when everybody surfaced at Squirrel Ashcraft's home in Evanston. Everybody who played in Chicago or even just passed through between the years 1930 and 1942 stopped for a while at Squirrel's to play or listen or maybe just relax. I managed to do a little of all three.

He had a house band that was always available. Jim McPartland played cornet. Orm Downes and Rosy McHargue from Ted Weems's band played drums and clarinet respectively, Bud Wilson was on trombone, Bill Priestley played guitar or the cornet Bix gave him, and Squirrel played piano. This group was frequently augmented by all the Bobcats or the Summa Cum Laude band. One night the entire Bob Crosby band came by and Squirrel proudly reported that the first complaint came from three blocks away and that between 8:00 P.M. and 9:00 A.M. three and one-half cases of scotch were consumed.

His informal sessions often threw unlikely musicians together. One night Brad Gowans and Joe Rushton just played duets and a valve trombone and bass saxophone is a strange combination but it sounded all right. On another night Bud and Pee Wee traded instruments and sounded like each other and on yet another night Bobby Hackett and Jimmy McPartland met for the first time. They kept their own mouthpieces but exchanged horns and played *Till We Meet Again* for about twenty minutes, exchanging choruses.

The meetings at Squirrel's also helped a lot of guys get jobs. It was a place where you could leave a message, a Plunkett's West if you will. Some bands were even born in the sessions and some that never played anywhere else were captured on home recordings. There are a lot of home recordings made by Jimmy McPartland's band that recorded for Decca that are easily as good as the ones that were later commercially released, and Bob Zurke made his only solo records at Squirrel's. You can hear Bix in him when he didn't have to play boogie-woogie.

The war closed down the house because Squirrel was in the navy, but I remember the good time, the bocce ball and the times I was left in charge at 4:00 A.M. on many Tuesday mornings.

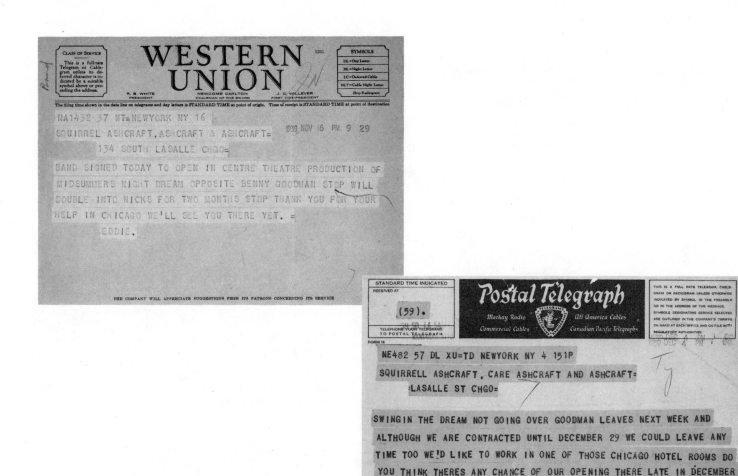

WESTERN UNION

CLASS OF SERVICE

This is a full-rate Telegram or Cable-gram unless its deferred character is indicated by a suitable symbol above or preceding the address.

R. B. WHITE
PRESIDENT

NEWCOMB CARLTON
CHAIRMAN OF THE BOARD

J. C. WILLEVER
FIRST VICE-PRESIDENT

SYMBOLS

DL=Day Letter
NL=Night Letter
LC=Deferred Cable
NLT=Cable Night Letter
Ship Radiogram

The filing time shown in the date line on telegrams and day letters is STANDARD TIME at point of origin. Time of receipt is STANDARD TIME at point of destination

NA1432 37 NT=NEWYORK NY 16

SQUIRREL ASHCRAFT,ASHCRAFT & ASHCRAFT=

134 SOUTH LASALLE CHGO=

1939 NOV 16 PM 9 29

BAND SIGNED TODAY TO OPEN IN CENTRE THEATRE PRODUCTION OF
MIDSUMMERS NIGHT DREAM OPPOSITE BENNY GOODMAN STOP WILL
DOUBLE INTO NICKS FOR TWO MONTHS STOP THANK YOU FOR YOUR
HELP IN CHICAGO WE'LL SEE YOU THERE YET. =

EDDIE.

THE COMPANY WILL APPRECIATE SUGGESTIONS FROM ITS PATRONS CONCERNING ITS SERVICE

Postal Telegraph

STANDARD TIME INDICATED
RECEIVED AT

(59).

TELEPHONE YOUR TELEGRAMS
TO POSTAL TELEGRAPH

FORM 14

Mackay Radio   All America Cables
Commercial Cables   Canadian Pacific Telegraphs

THIS IS A FULL RATE TELEGRAM, CABLE-GRAM OR RADIOGRAM UNLESS OTHERWISE INDICATED BY SYMBOL IN THE PREAMBLE OR IN THE ADDRESS OF THE MESSAGE. SYMBOLS DESIGNATING SERVICE SELECTED ARE OUTLINED IN THE COMPANY'S TARIFFS ON HAND AT EACH OFFICE AND ON FILE WITH REGULATORY AUTHORITIES.

NE482 57 DL XU=TD NEWYORK NY 4 151P

SQUIRRELL ASHCRAFT, CARE ASHCRAFT AND ASHCRAFT=

:LASALLE ST CHGO=

:SWINGIN THE DREAM NOT GOING OVER GOODMAN LEAVES NEXT WEEK AND
ALTHOUGH WE ARE CONTRACTED UNTIL DECEMBER 29 WE COULD LEAVE ANY
TIME TOO WE'D LIKE TO WORK IN ONE OF THOSE CHICAGO HOTEL ROOMS DO
YOU THINK THERES ANY CHANCE OF OUR OPENING THERE LATE IN DECEMBER
OR EARLY IN JANUARY QUERY REGARDS FROM THE FELLOWS=

:EDDIE CONDON.

In the Fall of 1939 a European producer, Erik Charell, presented a jazz version of A Midsummer Night's Dream. The Over Come Loaded was asked to play and we did for as long as the show was open, which was about three minutes. We played on one side of the stage in a small box and Benny Goodman was on the other side with one of his sextets. Don Vorhees was in the pit and Louis Armstrong was on stage with Maxine Sullivan. Our part in the show was cut down to a couple of numbers so we had a lot of time to sit around and watch the show die. This was the first time anybody tried to use jazz bands on the Broadway stage and they didn't know what they were doing. We did after the first night and we started scratching around to see where we could line up some work. Nick had fired us when he heard we were going on the legitimate stage and it looked like lean times. Squirrel Ashcraft helped save us and we were off to Chicago for a month in the Panther Room. It was the first time I was back in Chicago in almost a dozen years.

A *typical* session at Squirrel's, with Orm Downes, Jack Howe, Rosey McHargue, Spencer Clark, Jimmy McPartland, and the Buds, Freeman and Wilson.

JIMMY MC PARTLAND AND BOB ZURKE

ROSEY MC HARGUE, HOWARD KENNEDY, JIMMY MC PARTLAND, ORM DOWNES, SQUIRREL ASHCRAFT

Jimmy McPartland's regular band at Bill Priestley's house with Jack Gardner, Joe Rushton, Hank Issacs and Wade Foster in 1939. Only Boyce is missing.

JANE ASHCRAFT, ZUTTY, PEANUTS HUCKO, BOBBY HACKETT

We could always relax at Squirrel's. Sometimes we were too relaxed. Once Pee Wee passed out from too much drink and too little food. We carried him upstairs and put him in one of the bedrooms. He didn't look too good and we called a doctor. The doctor arrived, took one look at Pee Wee and without hesitation had a drink. He should have seen Pee Wee when he really looked bad.

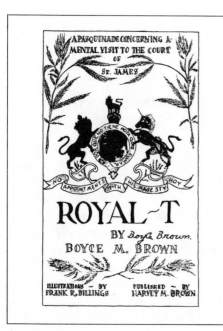

A PASQUINADE CONCERNING A MENTAL VISIT TO THE COURT OF ST. JAMES

ROYAL~T

BY *Boyce Brown.*

BOYCE M. BROWN

ILLUSTRATIONS ~ BY FRANK R. BILLINGS   PUBLISHED ~ BY HARVEY M. BROWN

In London, when I went to see King George the Fifth, his majesty, I learned that all of royalty smoke marijuana constantly; and they know what it's all about, I'll tell you how I found that out.

On entering the palace yard, a stiff, but silly looking guard who stood before the palace door said, "Halt, what have you come here for?" "I've come to see the king," I said, to which he grinned and shook his head.

Boyce Brown was a slow reader. He was blind in one eye and had about one-tenth vision in the other, but he was an intellectual who listened to Delius and wrote poetry. He was also religious and entered a monastery in the forties. He emerged from the monastery shortly before his death in the fifties. He appeared on a TV show and made a record with me called "Brother Matthew."

"You wish to see the King? - oh my, I'm sure he's somewhere getting - high, - but that is well - for when he's - down - he feels so mean, just yesterday he told the Queen - to go to hell. Of course she smokes the bloomin' stuff, she's given up the use of snuff, - though strange to tell.

"I," he continued, "can't begin to tell the state that England's in since royal heads are smoking, moot, it gives them such a blasted boot; not only that, our gracious King, has found out what it means to swing, since when each morn' at his command the hottest - six piece - negro band goes marching all through London town, and you should hear them break-it-down.

The King, arising, takes his throne and with his mighty slide - trombone he plays a strain from bugle blues which means, Sir James, what is the news? Sir James then answers him in song, he sings just like the great Armstrong, thus they converse the whole day long.

At each meet of the House of Lords I swear they almost come to swords discussing, whose band stomps the best.

The House of Commons is forlorn, they realize they're full of corn but they just can't get on to swing. Our prince, by Jove, gets so knocked-out he hardly knows what he's about, he smokes a most exclusive brand imported straight from Dixie - land, and -...

Often, passing, in his coach, he tosses me a little roach, why even now I am so numb I've quite forgot you've really come to see the King? Sir, all you need for entrance is a stick of weed!

-- Glossary --

Marijuana -- ganja - bhang - weed - a powerful form of hashish consisting of the dried tops of pistillate hemp plants; smoked like tobacco. (wed)
Moot - see above
Blasted Boot - kick - as in the pants.
Swing - to be executed by hanging.
Armstrong - a perspiring negro trumpet player, whose art is now prostituted.
Full of corn - corn fed - or in the Arcadian mode.
Vo-de-o - a lingual expression used by those full of corn not liqueur.
Stomp - refer - break it down.
Knocked-out - numb as after a blasted boot.
Roach - a partially smoked stick of weed - refer marijuana.
To refer marijuana.
Break it down - refer - stomp.
Numb - knocked out - high.
Down - not high, loaded, knocked out, or numb but that which happens after one goes up.

One hundred copies of this original edition have been printed and the plates destroyed this is No. 999 of the seventy five relayed for restricted distribution in various bindings.

Bix gave Bill Priestley a trumpet and Bill has played it well ever since, along with playing fine guitar. He was not a professional musician; architect Mies van der Rohe would not let him. Avery Sherry played alto with the Princeton Triangle Jazz Band along with Squirrel, Bill, and Herb Sanford. He didn't play professionally either. He spends his time owning Wisconsin. Jack Gardner played professionally and didn't own anything except a good reputation.

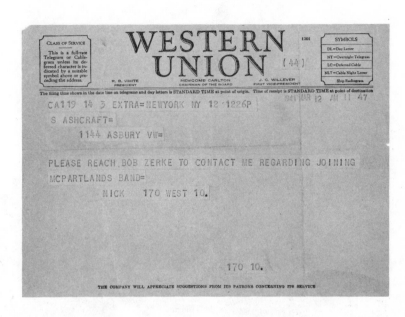

WESTERN UNION

(Above) This is a helluva duet. I played with Frank Signorelli from the late twenties into the thirties, but never associated with Bob much except at Squirrel's. He didn't last long enough to associate with anyone. Bob was a barrelhouse guy but Frank was the kind of player you could hire for any kind of a date and I once took him to a fancy dress ball at Otto Kahn's home on Long Island. He still lives in Brooklyn. Bob died in the mid-forties. His last job was driving an elevator.

(RIGHT) JOE RUSHTON, MIFF MOLE, STUFF SMITH, AND GEORGE WETTLING ON THE BANDSTAND

Stuff Smith is usually associated with the Onyx Club on Fifty-Second Street, but he made his way to Chicago and even alternated with our band at the Panther Room. Miff must have been up to something here. All eyes are on him.

Joe Rushton, a desperado in every sense, sitting on his favorite motorcycle at Squirrel's. He played metal clarinet and was the best bass saxophone player since Adrian Rollini. Joe once loaned Pee Wee his clarinet when Pee Wee broke his on a job in Chicago. Pee Wee was sometimes forgetful and when the job in Chicago was over he took the clarinet back with him to New York. Later, when Joe found out about it, he got on his motorcycle and drove nonstop from Chicago to New York. Pee Wee was playing at Nick's at the time and when Joe got there he was on the stand taking a solo. Joe walked right up to the bandstand and yanked the clarinet out of Pee Wee's permanently trembling hands. He said simply, "Pee Wee, that wasn't very nice." Joe walked out, got on his cycle, and scooted right back to Chicago. A year or so later Pee Wee came back to Chicago and met Joe at Squirrel's home in Evanston, the first suburb north of the city. Almost as soon as he arrived Pee Wee announced that he had to return very quickly to Chicago. Joe said he would take Pee Wee downtown. Imagine Pee Wee riding on the back of Joe's motorcycle for more than three feet, let alone all the way into Chicago. Pee Wee was never the same. Neither was Joe's bike.

Jack Gardner, the composer of "Bye Bye Pretty Baby." Sometimes he played with Harry James and other big bands. He should have played alone more often.

Town Hall

I was in and out of Nick's for most of 1941. Mostly out. During my waking hours Ernie Anderson and I would sit around and scheme. By the end of the year Ernie had convinced me that it was time to put real jazz in a concert hall. There had been a few concerts around town in places like Carnegie Hall, but they were swing band affairs where a lot of talented guys would sit down and play arrangements that someone else had written. There was room for a solo or two with the big bands but I was interested in real jazz, and Ernie thought that one or two customers might want to hear the real thing as well.

Ernie decided we should go into Carnegie Hall and together we persuaded Fats Waller to be our first attraction. No scored music, just real jazz. Fats was a great guy when it came to writing a score, but he seldom played one and was a perfect selection. The concert was set for 14 January 1942 and it was a solo effort for Fats with a few other guys thrown in to liven up the occasion. Paul Smith designed a poster, Phyllis wrote the flyer (Fats signed them all by hand), John Hammond wrote an appreciation, and we had our first jazz concert in Carnegie Hall. It was also the first time a black jazz artist ever headlined there.

Fats was perhaps a little nervous at the concert and he had a drink with every well-wisher in sight. He looked as far as he could to find them. I think he played "Summertime" about a dozen times in the second half of the program and his gold watch chain was forever falling out of his pocket—he had a watch chain that went all the way to his knees and it kept banging on the piano bench, particularly when he was sitting. Nobody seemed to mind about this, however, and the concert was an unqualified success. We went in with a band of our own later and started a series of concerts that lasted off and on into the sixties.

Sometime later we moved to Town Hall. It was less formal and was not so cavernous. It was also cheaper. It had to be because the most we took in at any of the three concerts that season was $516.75. But Ernie and I were game and decided to come back in the fall with a concert every month. We knew we had a good idea and were determined to be successful— if only to get our money back.

Ernie and I came back in November ready to try again. I had been working for Uncle Sam all summer doing what I could playing camps and making radio transcriptions and the relative security of Town Hall was just right for a quick change of pace. We didn't change anything except the size of the audience and it got bigger and bigger until there were people standing in the street. Even the critics were kind. Virgil Thomson ended his review of our first concert with the comment that "the nine-part tuttis were of a grandeur, a sumptuousness of sound and a spontaneous integration of individual freedoms that makes one proud of the country that gave birth to such a high manifestation of sensibility and intelligence, and happy to be present at such a full and noble expression of the musical faculties."

As the concerts became more popular we branched out. We took them on the road, we had a radio broadcast every Saturday, and we even televised a few. We even had special concerts in Carnegie Hall and the Ritz Theater. But the years during the war were best, until I put the guys on a regular television series at NBC in 1947.

THE TOWN HALL

 123 WEST 43rd STREET, NEW YORK, N. Y.

Eddie Condon Presents

By Johnny De Vries

A JAZZ CONCERT
Decembet Eighteenth, Nineteen Forty-three

ALFRED SCOTT · PUBLISHER · 156 FIFTH AVENUE, NEW YORK
82-12-18A-43

THE TOWN HALL
SEASON 1943-1944

FIRE NOTICE:—Look around NOW and choose the nearest Exit to your seat. In case of fire walk (not run) to THAT Exit. Do not try to beat your neighbor to the street.
PATRICK WALSH, *Fire Commissioner*

Saturday Afternoon, December 18th, at 5:30 o'clock
ERNEST ANDERSON *presents a*

JAZZ CONCERT

Directed by EDDIE CONDON

THE MUSICIANS:

PIANISTS: Joe Bushkin, Mel Powell
DRUMMERS: Sidney Catlett, George Wettling
CORNETISTS: Bobby Hackett, Max Kaminsky
CLARINETISTS: Edmund Hall, Peewee Russell
TROMBONISTS: Lou McGarrity, Benny Morton
BASSIST: Bob Casey
GUITARIST AND CONDUCTOR: Eddie Condon

VOCALIST: Miss Lee Wiley

In order to preserve the unrestrained ad lib qualities of this music, the artists may depart from the following program at any time.

A *Commodore record date*, 1941. An orchestral group featuring Messrs. Bushkin, Wettling, Casey, Kaminsky, Russell, McGarrity and Condon.

1. Strut Miss Lizzie
2. Ballin' the Jack
3. I ain't gonna give nobody none of my Jellyroll . . .
   which includes a solo by Mr. Peewee Russell.

Program Continued on Second Page Following

PROGRAM NOTE FOR EDDIE CONDON'S SECOND JAZZ CONCERT

FOR THE 1944 SEASON

JANUARY 8, 5:30 P.M.

12/28/43 - GS

I am sorry to report that people are beginning to bring thermometers
to Eddie Condon's concerts, to measure the exact degree of heat they give off.
This is really a tribute to the group, but it has its dangers, too. That's the
way people used to listen to Caruso - trying to assay the exact percentage of
gold in the voice on Tuesday night compared with last Thursday. I suppose it's
the way people watched Nijinsky, counting his entrechats to see if he'd hit ten
again.

This sort of watchfulness implies that the musical virtuosi here
assembled are the best in the batch - because they are their own standard, and
all others (including themselves, so to speak) are measured by them. The danger
is that this fluid ensemble will begin to get rigid and self-conscious. It's no
use trying to get hot - you're either hot or you aren't playing around here.

The average citizen doesn't measure heat - he reacts to it. So
the Maestro (a Mr. Condon) and the impresario (a Mr. Anderson) needn't worry too
much. They'll have an audience - not as big as their merits deserve - but appreciative.

Listening to a lot of hot music recorded in the late '30's is an
exciting experience. Listening to Eddie's boys as they work right in front of you
is even better. There's a feeling that at any moment a master-work may be created
and if it is, will never be heard again. It happens often enough to make these
arranged jam-sessions among the fine musical events of the season.

Additional notes: 1) Virgil Thomson seems to be not only a pioneer but still the only *(one of the few)* daily-paper critic to understand the significance of what's going on here. 2) Many of the old recordings listed above indicate that monotony is an important element in good jazz production. If I get asked to write the program note for the February 19th concert, I'll report further.

3) I say nothing about the personal attractiveness of Condon or any of the surrounding geniuses. But this might be worth looking into: a good small hot combo is better picture material than any 99 men (without the girl). Condon is no Stokowski in looks, but we used to put on a good television show with him and his pals and pictorially, as well as musically, it was terrific.

Gilbert Seldes

GILBERT SELDES PROGRAM NOTE

Gilbert usually gave me the best of everything, including giving me my first shot on TV.

SWING WITHOUT WORDS

by GILBERT SELDES

*A program note written on the occasion of
the first Jazz Concert of the 1942 season*

It is a remarkable thing that the vocabulary of swing became popular faster than swing itself. People who turned off the radio when anything hotter than 1924 Whiteman was played, still found the jargon of superjazz an enchantment all by itself. It sounded tough, terribly knowing, and sophisticated to talk about gut-bucket, solid sending, and the like. And at the same time a vast sentimentality rose over swing, hot jazz and jitterbugs. It is almost as if we were getting emotional about young men in war; only it happened before we were in the war.

We all do this sort of thing in one way or another — and we obscure what we are trying to illuminate by our words. I have written about the style of an outfielder and Mr. Ernest Hemingway finds something priestly and austere in a second baseman whom I have never observed. In an odd way, we are press agents. The only thing words can do for music is also to press-agent, to write an invitation, to make you want to listen and prepare you, so you will not be too hostile to what you hear.

According to the management, you will hear a Jazz Concert. Mr. Paul Whiteman gave a concert of what he called Jazz in 1924. Maybe his concert was the end of ragtime and this one is true jazz; maybe his was jazz and this is swing. The one immediate difference I can see between the 1924 concert (for which I wrote a few program notes) and today is that a lot of the music we called jazz in 1924 was still derived from song, a lot more was meant for dancing — and only a little was to be heard (Zez Confrey's *Kitten on the Keys,* Gershwin's *Rhapsody*). Today, the music played by Eddie Condon's band is meant to be heard — and if you are a prime jitterbug you can dance to it, but that is secondary. This may not make any ultimate difference to American music; but it makes listening more rewarding. Your ear gets more

for its money, so to speak. You follow a complex structure instead of a merely complicated pattern; you are kept interested.

When I was defending jazz — from the critics, not the people — I was told that *all* popular songs were alike — that *all* jazz was the same. I never knew what that meant; popular songs always had so many bars of theme, so many of middle section, so many of repeat; and apparently serious musicians found that boresome. But to me there was infinite variety in Donaldson and Berlin and Hirsch and Kern; and all the difference in the world between Whiteman and Lopéz and Ellington and Emil Coleman. Today swing seems to break out of all the grooves and masterly improvisations afford surprise and novelty all the way. I don't know what the critics think of swing, but I should suppose that any composer would delight in the virtuosity of its players.

Today's concert brings Bix Beiderbecke's name in as a composer; and it recalls his already legendary figure in another way: the band includes two top-flight cornetists (Kaminsky and Hackett) — two, because no one cornetist can do all the things Beiderbecke did.

The players, as you will gather, are working men. They work in other bands and orchestras. They *play* here.

November 4th, 1942   —GILBERT SELDES

Two years later Gilbert was still writing about us.

THOSE JAZZ CONCERTS

The next event on the agenda is *Bud Freeman's* concert in TOWN HALL, Thursday evening, December 27th at 8:30. Eddie Condon and Ernie Anderson will present this recital with some additional dialogue by Pete Pesci. The cast will include people like *Joe Bushkin, Cliff Jackson, Billy Butterfield, George Wettling* and a half a dozen others. We've saved the best locations at this concert for the crowd at Eddie Condon's, so if you want tickets tell your waiter and he'll get them for you. $1.20, 1.80, 2.40, & 3.60.

* * *

☞ The first Saturday of every month means Eddie Condon is at TOWN HALL. Next concert January 5th at 5:30. Ask your waiter for tickets.

* * *

Eddie will stage his final eliminations at a special CARNEGIE HALL concert early in 1946.

* * *

YOU CAN'T TELL THE PHOTOGRAPHERS
WITHOUT A SCORECARD!

Eastman is going to declare a dividend on the strength of our opening. Among those scheduled to be on the premises that night are GJON MILI of Life, LISETTE MODEL of Harper's Bazaar, OTTO HESS of Liberty, WEEGEE of Julius', SKIPPY ADELMAN of Black Star, SAM SIEGAL of the Office of War Information, & SAM ANDRE of Pic.

* * *

☞ *Charles Peterson* is the man responsible for those photographs in the bar. A musician turned photographer, Charlie has followed the activities of the barefoot mob since 1927.

* * *

☞ Listen to Fred Robbins, WOV, 1280 on your dial, every night except Sunday from 7:30 to 10:00. Then come right over!

* * *

☞ *Milt Gabler* was the pioneer responsible for some of the best recordings of this kind of music. His COMMODORE label includes excellent specimens of the work of virtually every player you're likely to hear here. And his Commodore Music Shop, 136 East 42nd Street, New York, is where we buy all our records.

* * *

ANDY is our head bartender. NICK is our head waiter. And ALBERT is our chef. They're all nice guys.

* * *

Address all complaints to Eddie Condon's, 47 West Third St., New York City, 12. If you want to get future issues of THE BLOTTER leave your name and address with Pete.

* * *

**Eddie Condon's was designed by RUSSELL PATTERSON
and executed by DICK WALTER.**

E. M. DIAMANT, 191 LEXINGTON AVENUE, SETS ALL OUR TYPE. QUAKER PRESS, 118 WEST 22d STREET, PRINTS IT. PAUL SMITH IS OUR ART DIRECTOR.

The EDDIE CONDON BLOTTER

VOL. 1 NO. 1   DECEMBER, 1945

THE CAST OF CHARACTERS on the bandstand are: (left to right) *Gene Schroeder*, late of Nick's; *The Proprietor* and his pork chop; *Wild Bill Davison*, the Chicago trumpeter; *Joe Marsala*, the Musicraft recording artist; *Brad Gowans*, valve trombonist and center fielder for the Arlington Billionaires; *Bob Casey*, the basey; and *Dave Tough*, the mite that's right at night.

* * *

Our piano soloist (he picked out the Steinway himself) is none other than *Joe Sullivan*.

* * *

We are sorry to report that there is no JULIUS' in the immediate vicinity. However, barring drifts, it's only a ten minute walk. (On a clear day you can see Bill Kennedy's overcoat from our front stoop.)

* * *

Our New Year's Eve policy is:

BONDED RESERVATIONS ONLY

There will be a three dollar cover and no four o'clock curfew. Better speak to Pete right now. (Pete Pesci, GR 3-8736.)

* * *

Where's Jack Bland?

* * *

☞ Have you heard Decca's new Eddie Condon album? It's a George Gershwin Jazz Concert, Americondon style. Pete Pesci bought one.

WHAT HAPPENS ON MONDAY NIGHTS?

Monday night is Smithsonian Night at Eddie Condon's. Bring your own bell jar. *Bud Freeman*, the Aleutian tenor saxophonist, will conduct the proceedings. Monday, December 23rd, his staff will include such people as BOBBY HACKETT, GEORGE WETTLING, BOB HAGGART, DAVE BOWMAN, JOE DIXON, VERNON BROWN, and CARMEN MASTREN. Piano solos will be by former Master Sergeant JOE BUSHKIN, providing he arrives in from Guam on schedule. Added starters may include Billy Butterfield and Ernie Caceres.

The murals that aren't up yet are by Johnny DeVries, we think.

* * *

THOSE WOR MICROPHONES simply mean that Eddie is broadcasting a new series from the club on the Mutual's coat-to-vest network. Looks like Fred Robbins, of WOV's 1280 Club, will be our announcer.

The first two blotters for our last season. These were left on the tables at Julius's and my club and anywhere else we could leave them. Johnny De Vries was responsible for the drawing and my wife Phyllis and Paul Smith helped put together the copy.

The EDDIE CONDON BLOTTER

VOL. I   January, 1946   No. 2

THIS is the fifth January since The Barefoot Mob first brought free-wheeling AMERICONDON music into the New York concert halls. Our first Town Hall audience was so scant that EDDIE addressed it as: *Lady and Gentleman*. On several later occasions the musicians on the stage outnumbered the paying customers.

Some of the critics thought that CONDON, ANDERSON & Co. should be committed, and it must be stated here that in some quarters this opinion still prevails. Others, however, thought these recitals a lively and interesting idea and they encouraged them.

It is this encouragement that you must thank or blame for the fact that these concerts still persist.

THE BLOTTER is the program for the first EDDIE CONDON JAZZ CONCERT of 1946. If this kind of entertainment pleases you, see your doctor immediately. If it does not, then forward your complaint to JOHN CHAPMAN, EMILY COLEMAN, GEORGE FRAZIER, WILDER HOBSON, IRVING KOLODIN, GILBERT SELDES, ROBERT SIMON, ROGERS WHITTAKER, and VIRGIL THOMSON. They are the responsible parties. They encouraged us and they probably knew what they were doing. The defense rests.

Eddie Condon Presents

A Jazz Concert

IN TOWN HALL, SAT. AFTERNOON, JAN. 5th AT 5:30

N. B. Eddie Condon conducts a jazz concert in Town Hall on the first Saturday of every month, October through May. (Associated with him in this enterprise are: Ernest Anderson, Pete Pesci, Johnny O'Connor, George Carhart, Joe Bamberger, Wm. Kennedy, Arthur Prale and Ralph Krud. Exploitation is under the exclusive direction of Harold Fitzsimmons.)

THE PLAYERS

Pianists: JOE BUSHKIN, JOE SULLIVAN & GENE SCHROEDER; *Drummers:* DAVE TOUGH & GEORGE WETTLING; *Bassists:* BOB HAGGART & SID WEISS; *Trumpeters:* WILD BILL DAVISON & BILLY BUTTERFIELD; *Clarinetists:* ED HALL, TONY PARENTI & JOE DIXON; *Trombonists:* BRAD GOWANS & GEORGE BRUNIES; *Guitarist & Conductor:* EDDIE CONDON. *Program Anotator:* FRED ROBBINS.

Our saxophone section, Bud Freeman and Sidney Bechet, is in sick bay this week. If either or both are well enough they will be on hand this afternoon.

A Program Note

Written for the Town Hall concert of February 19th, 1944, when it was first announced that the Blue Network had signed Eddie for a series of programs.

They say that EDDIE CONDON and his boy geniuses are going on the air. And if you ask him, he may tell you how and for whom and when. I'll only tell you why.

This aggregation of talent has a special style and quality — not only musically but as a production. That quality comes in the first place from EDDIE himself. How he will manage to walk around and make those comments on the air, I don't know. He'll drive a few radio engineers and directors crazy. But he'll put *his* music *over*.

Of course the sauntering and unrehearsed quality of the TOWN HALL JAZZ CONCERTS isn't their prime value. The music is the thing — and the CONDON boys seem to have hit on a mixture of elements that is just right. It highlights the remarkable specialists — but usually the ensembles are sustained and interesting. These people are co-workers, not collaborationists.

In the notes for the previous program I threatened to write something about monotony as the basis of good swing music. But I thought launching EDDIE and the boys on the air was more interesting. Maybe next time.

GILBERT SELDES

The PROGRAM

In order to preserve the unrestrained ad lib qualities of this music the artists may depart from the following program at any time.

I

THE BAND AT EDDIE CONDON'S

Four tunes that sounded good last night, played by the orchestra from the new gymnasium at 47 West 3rd Street.

II

BETWEEN SETS AT EDDIE CONDON'S

JOE SULLIVAN, the interim soloist at 47 West 3rd Street, plays his own composition, GIN MILL BLUES (*Better phone Pete for your reservation right now. GR 3-8736*).

III

MONDAY NIGHT AT EDDIE CONDON'S

The Monday night orchestra, directed by BUD FREEMAN, plays some Aleutian folk music.

An intermission of eight minutes

IV

THE RETURN OF JOE BUSHKIN

The Satan of the Steinway, lately returned from an engagement at LOEW'S TOKYO, plays his own variations on familiar songs.

V

SITTING IN AT EDDIE CONDON'S

A collective improvisation by the entire company. Following the concert, the culprits will repair to EDDIE CONDON'S (47 West 3rd Street, GR 3-8736, a block below Washington Square, a step from the 4th Street Station of the Independent Subway System) to discuss this afternoon's music and to play some more. Basket parties are welcome.

☞ EDDIE'S next concert in this hall takes place on Saturday afternoon, February 2nd at 5:30. If you're reading this at EDDIE CONDON'S (47 W. 3rd St.) or at JULIUS' (Waverly at 10th St.) your waiter can get you seats. ($2.40 each).

* * *

☞ FRED ROBBINS may be heard nightly, except Sundays, on Station WOV, 1280 Kc. on your dial. Are you a member of the 1280 Club?

* * *

☞ JEROME CARGILL, of the A. & S. Lyons office, 515 Madison Avenue, New York City, is booking the Condon Troup for jazz concerts throughout the East on Monday nights beginning February 4th. On that date Eddie will make his first appearance in WORCESTER, MASSACHUSETTS. Subsequent Mondays will see The Barefoot Mob in BALTIMORE, WASHINGTON, BOSTON, PHILADELPHIA, BUFFALO, CLEVELAND, ROCHESTER, COLUMBUS, SYRACUSE, ALBANY, HARTFORD, BRIDGEPORT, PITTSBURGH, and other cities

* * *

DECCA & COMMODORE RECORDS   STEINWAY PIANOS

* * *

Where's Jack Bland?

MUSIC

Jazz at 5:30

It is about time that lovers of hot music had a chance to listen to it in comfortable seats, without getting sinus trouble, and free from the compulsion to get funky with cut whisky at speakeasy prices.

So wrote an avid amateur jazz musician, Paul Smith, in a Manhattan jazz concert program note a month ago. Last week Manhattanites had their fourth chance of the season to hear jazz—authentic, impromptu jazz—in the plush seats of Town Hall.

On the stage were some of the greatest of jazz improvisers: gaunt, lean-fingered "Pee Wee" Russell, famed for his hoarse clarinet tones; bobbing, supple-wristed

Phonograph companies have practically stopped issuing hot jazz records. If jazz could be given the needle, Guitarist Condon was the man to do it. An oldtime member of Chicago's Austin High gang, he organized bands for the first great jazz records of the Chicago school in 1927. Ever since he has been a catalyst of jazz, who never takes a chorus himself.

Last week's slim audience didn't bother Eddie Condon. Nor did it discourage his backer, bespectacled Ernest Anderson, onetime adman and CBS executive. For next season he has arranged eleven biweekly Town Hall jazz concerts for Eddie Condon, with more possibly to come, at the same unseasonal (for jazz) hour as last week's: 5:30 p.m.

Vern-Swift

EDDIE CONDON & THE BOYS*
Nobody got sinus or cut whiskey.

Zutty Singleton and round-faced "Kansas," ace Negro drummers; Trombonists Benny Morton and Jay C. Higginbotham; bright-eyed "Hot Lips" Page and tiny Max Kaminsky; Bassist Billy Taylor; James P. Johnson, veteran Negro hot pianist. Twelve in all took turns. Unceremonious master of ceremonies was assertive, sharp-jawed Eddie Condon, who did what leading was done while he strummed his guitar.

What the concert aimed to do was to revivify a form of popular music which had lately become much less popular. In the 1920s, when jazz flourished in Chicago, there used to be great jam sessions in hotspots after closing time. By 1936 hot jazz had weaned a commercially successful but adulterated form of itself: swing. Today, it is commercial swing and the smooth, symphonic arrangements of name bands that make big money and attract jitterbugs.

With Fife & Drum

Tin Pan Alley was still grinding its own powder for the war this week, but mostly its powder looked and smelled like corn meal:

► Some of the song titles: *Our Glorious America, Defend Your Country, There's Millions of Yankees On Their Way, Buckle Down Buck Private.*

► The flock of MacArthur songs still poured out. Among them: *Here's To You, MacArthur; Hats Off to MacArthur, We've Got a Wonder Down Under.* What sounded the most sincere and tuneful: *Fightin' Doug MacArthur.*

► Lyric Writer Bud Green had a new twist, but little else, in his *On the Old Assembly Line*, to Ray Henderson's music. End of the chorus:

* Billy Taylor, Condon, "Pee Wee" Russell, Jay C. Higginbotham, Zutty Singleton.

Our first concert in Town Hall was poorly attended. About the only person there was the guy from Time.

88

I'm gonna sit right down and write yourself a letter ...

About a gr8 d8 that's definitely on the s18, for about half past 8 on January 14th.

You see, on this d8, there's going to be a deb8, (well, a sort of t8-a-t8,) between this humble advoc8 of the piano laure8, and a few intim8 sk8s. (Friends, by the way, of the L8 Sister K8.)

It'll be at Carnegie Hall.

I'd like to prognostic8 - it's going to be some conglomer8 of that brand of vertebr8 that loves to gravit8 around a musical cr8 and a str8-bar-8 and start to cre8...good music!

Most of the evening I'll be playing a Steinway grand and a Hammond organ. But some of the time Artie Shaw and Gene Krupa and Eddie Condon and some other marvelous musicians will be helping out by sitting in.

Don't forget the d8, 75 cents to 2 dollars plus tax pays the fr8. By the way don't be L8.

See you at the g8,

Fats

Fats Waller, 88*

*The first 88 keys are the hardest.

THE FLYER FOR THE FATS WALLER CONCERT

FATS AT THE CONCERT

THE INTERMISSION BAND FOR FATS, WITH BUD, JOHN KIRBY, GENE KRUPA, MAX KAMINSKY, AND PEE WEE

THE TOWN HALL

123 WEST 43rd STREET, NEW YORK, N. Y.

Eddie Condon Presents

By Johnny De Vries

A JAZZ CONCERT
April Eighth, Nineteen Forty-four

ALFRED SCOTT · PUBLISHER · 156 FIFTH AVENUE, NEW YORK
211-1-8A-44

THE TOWN HALL
SEASON 1943-1944

FIRE NOTICE — Look around now and choose the nearest exit to your seat. In case of fire walk (not run) to *that* Exit. Do not try to beat your neighbor to the street.

PATRICK WALSH, *Fire Commissioner.*

Saturday Afternoon, April 8th, at 5:30 o'clock

ERNEST ANDERSON presents a

JAZZ CONCERT

Directed by EDDIE CONDON

THE MUSICIANS:

PIANISTS: James P. Johnson, Gene Schroeder, Joe Bushkin
DRUMMERS: Kansas, Cosy Cole, Sidney Catlett, George Wettling, Joe Grauso, Dave Tough
CORNETISTS: Bobby Hackett, Max Kaminsky, Bill Coleman, Muggsy Spanier
CLARINETISTS: Edmund Hall, Peewee Russell, Ernie Caceres
TROMBONISTS: Miff Mole, Benny Morton
BASSISTS: Oscar Pettiford, Bob Casey
GUITARIST AND CONDUCTOR: Eddie Condon

★ ★ ★

VOCALIST: Red McKenzie

In order to preserve the unrestrained ad lib qualities of this music, the artists may depart from the following program at any time.

Program Continued on Second Page Following

The program said that "in order to preserve the unrestrained ad lib qualities of this music, the artists may depart from the following program . . ." We always did.

EDDIE CONDON

SUBSCRIPTION SERIES, 5:30 SATURDAY AFTERNOONS, **NOVEMBER 4,**
DECEMBER 2 AND **JANUARY 20,** AND CHRISTMAS AFTERNOON,
DECEMBER 25.
PRESENTING MORE THAN FIFTY OF THE
GREATEST JAZZ MUSICIANS OF OUR TIME **CARNEGIE HALL**

SUBSCRIPTION PRICE SCHEDULE
(All Prices Include Tax)

Orchestra or Box Seat for 4 Concerts at $2.50............$8.00
Dress Circle Seat for 4 Concerts at $1.80...................$6.00
Balcony Seat for 4 Concerts at $1.20........................$3.60

Seats Purchased for Individual Concerts
$1.20—$2.50 for Saturdays and
$1.20—$3.00 for Christmas Day

EDDIE CONDON
JANUARY 20th SATURDAY AFTERNOON AT 5:30

PRESENTING MORE THAN THIRTY OF THE
GREATEST JAZZ MUSICIANS OF OUR TIME **CARNEGIE HALL**

This will be Mr. Condon's final New York Concert this season.

All seats reserved — $1.20 to $2.50 including tax.

Eddie Condon

WILL CONDUCT A JAZZ CONCERT
CHRISTMAS DAY, DECEMBER 25th
AT 5:30 P. M.
FEATURING 40 OF THE
GREATEST HOT MUSICIANS OF OUR TIME.

Carnegie Hall

ALL SEATS RESERVED—$1.20 to $3.00 Tax Incl.

Since many were turned away at Eddie's last concert because of limited box office facilities, you are urged to get your seats as far in advance as possible.

PIANISTS: GENE SCHROEDER, JESS STACY, ART HODES, CLIFF JACKSON, HARRY GIBSON, SAM PRICE, CLYDE HART; TRUMPETERS: MAX KAMINSKY, BOBBY HACKETT, MUGGSY SPANIER, BILLY BUTTERFIELD, BILL COLEMAN, YANK LAUSON, WINGY MANONE; DRUMMERS: COZY COLE, DAVE TOUGH, AL SIDELL, GEORGE WETTLING, JOE GRAUSO, DANNY ALVIN, KANSAS; TROMBONISTS: MIFF MOLE, LOU McGARITY, BENNY MORTON, BILL HARRIS, TOMMY DORSEY; CLARINETISTS: SIDNEY BECHET, EDMOND HALL, PEEWEE RUSSELL, WOODY HERMAN, ERNIE CACERES, JOE MARSALA; BASSISTS: JACK LESBERG, BOB HAGGART, SID WEISS, BOB CASEY; SINGER: LEE WILEY; GUITARIST & CONDUCTOR: EDDIE CONDON.

THE JAZZ CONCERT SOCIETY
ANNOUNCES A SERIES OF FOUR
Jazz Concerts
DIRECTED BY EDDIE CONDON
BEGINNING
SATURDAY AFTERNOON AT 5:30 P. M.
DECEMBER 18th

AT TOWN HALL — 113 WEST 43rd STREET — ALL SEATS RESERVED — $1.10 and $1.65

THIS OPENING PROGRAM WILL FEATURE PIANO DUETS BY JOE BUSHKIN AND MEL POWELL. OTHER SOLOISTS WILL INCLUDE BOBBY HACKETT, MAX KAMINSKY, PEEWEE RUSSELL, EDMUND HALL, GEORGE WETTLING, SIDNEY CATLETT, LOU McGARRITY, BENNY MORTON AND OTHER FAMOUS COMMODORE RECORDING ARTISTS.

We had a mailing list all over the country because of the radio broadcasts. We sent postcards all the way to California and a few people from there probably showed up.

THE JAZZ CONCERT SOCIETY
announces a series of four

Jazz Concerts

Directed by EDDIE CONDON

At TOWN HALL • 113 West 43rd Street, New York City
All Seats Reserved • $1.10 and $1.65

SATURDAY AFTERNOONS *at* 5:30 P. M.
DECEMBER 18th • JANUARY 8th • FEBRUARY 19th • MARCH 11th

"IMPROVISING by our greatest instrumentalists under EDDIE CONDON's *direction* has provided the most absorbing musical experience that I have been through in some years, and one of the highest manifestations of the musical faculties it has ever been my pleasure to witness."

Virgil Thompson

A good ad, but why the Park Lane photo?

MUSIC

Roosevelt Epic

The Yugoslavs who for centuries have chanted endless epic ballads about their heroes now have new heroes and new epics.

Draja Mihailovich's Chetniks now have a song that describes a heroic drinking bout between Winston Churchill and Joseph Stalin. After downing oceans of red wine they decide to send a message of hope to Douglas MacArthur.

Another song is about two heroes riding their chargers triumphantly through the Bosnian mountains. Sample stanzas:

Mountain speaks to mountain:
Why are you, mountain, full of shade?
Why are you silent today?
Did you not see who rode through you?

They are neither wedding guests nor
rich people,
But two brave comrades:
Mihailovich the gallant knight,
And, next to him, none other than
Roosevelt.
They are riding two black steeds,
And are afraid of no one. . . .

Then Mihailovich speaks to Roosevelt:
Listen to me, comrade:
Who cares for your cattle at home?
Who looks after your vineyards?

And Roosevelt replies:
Hush! Be still, brave knight.
The cattle are perishing from lack of
care;
The vineyards are neglected.
But four sons I've raised, on sugar and
silk,
All four I've sent to the four corners of
the world,
To fight the four czars.
God will grant that they crush them. . . .

Jive for Epicures

U.S. jive epicures consider the jazz played by such famous name bands as Tommy Dorsey's or Glenn Miller's a low, commercial product. Their heroes are unsung swingsters who improvise nightly for a favored few in hotspots like Chicago's College Inn, Manhattan's Nick's. Their treasured classics are discs made in the '20s by such Chicago immortals as the late Leon ("Bix") Beiderbecke and King Oliver's Creole Jazz Band.

Last week at Manhattan's Town Hall, Guitarist Eddie Condon and a group of top-flight jazz artists inaugurated a bimonthly series of jive concerts cooked to the epicure's taste, proved to their own satisfaction that the grand tradition of the "Chicago Style" is as alive as ever. At the opening concert Pianist Mel Powell, Trombonist Benny Morton, Cornetist Bobby Hackett, Drummer Zutty Singleton got off to a methodical start, ended in an inspired jam session. The audience of epicures (who consider it sacrilege to dance to jive) sat rapt in their seats. By the time the players were really hitting their stride, Town Hall's furniture movers started clearing the stage for another concert. The players kept right on playing. Only the ringing of an alarm bell stopped them. When Guitarist Condon asked the audience whether it wanted a second concert, it roared Yes.

So did the *Herald Tribune's* long-haired Critic Virgil Thomson. Said he next day: "The nine-part tuttis were of a grandeur, a sumptuousness of sound and a spontaneous integration of individual freedoms that makes one proud of the country that gave birth to such a high manifestation of sensibility and intelligence and happy to be present at such a full and noble expression of the musical faculties."

There was less sumptuousness of sound from Manhattan's jive epicures. Classicists from Nick's, who stickle for the traditions of the Chicago Style, nodded their heads in austere approval. But the Romantics from Café Society, who prefer the smoother, pianistic blues (boogie-woogie) of Meade Lux Lewis, turned their noses up. Said their crop-haired angel, John Henry Hammond Jr., about the Condonites: "They're working toward an artistic dead end. . . . About five years ago they reached a stage of musical sophistication that predicted a revolution in modern music, but they stopped there."

But Classicist Condon is undaunted. With the financial help of jive-struck Ernest Anderson, assistant vice president of D'Arcy Advertising Co., Condon hopes to make Manhattan's Town Hall a temple of pre-boogie-woogie tradition. Angel Anderson, like Classicist Condon, thinks Angel Hammond's barrel-shaped maestros of boogie-woogie are modernistic and monotonous. He is willing to risk $6,000 this season on Town Hall concerts to prove the superiority of the Chicago Style.

White Christmas

I'm dreaming of a White Christmas,
Just like the ones I used to know
Where the tree tops glisten And children
*listen to hear sleigh bells in the snow.**

Tailored by Tunesmith Irving Berlin for the suave, sleepy voice of Cinemactor Bing Crosby, this song (from Paramount's *Holiday Inn*) originally expressed the longing for sleet and ice of an Easterner marooned among the palm trees of Hollywood. But with thousands of U.S. servicemen facing snowless Christmases from North Africa to Guadalcanal, *White Christmas* has unexpectedly become the first big sentimental song hit of World War II.

Result: a sale, up to last week, of 600,000 copies—more (for a similar ten-week period) than any previous hit in Irving Berlin's hit-studded career.

Watching *White Christmas'* sales mount,
*Copyrighted by Irving Berlin Inc.

ANGEL ANDERSON & GUITARIST CONDON
For nine-part tuttis, $6,000.

Charles Peterson

In November 1942 business began to get better.

HOW TO LEAD A TWENTY-PIECE BAND

The Mad Mexican, Ernie Caceres

If Muggsy and Lips had stuck around longer the World's Greatest
Jazz Band might have had four trumpets.

No place but Town Hall. Muggsy Spanier and Tommy Dorsey.

SIDNEY BECHET AND KANSAS FIELDS

George looks evil today

A strange trio: Bob Casey, Kansas Fields, Sid Weiss

The Clarinet chase with Ernie, Pee Wee, and Joe

Just before the Gershwin Concert

JONAH JONES

JESS STACY

BENNY MORTON

Pee Wee's not unhappy here

Gene and I back in tails

BENNY MORTON, JONAH JONES, BILLY BUTTERFIELD, BOBBY HACKETT

GENE KRUPA

PEE WEE RUSSELL AND THE TWO ERNIES, CACERES AND ANDERSON

Visiting Jimmy Dorsey backstage at the Capitol Theater

Bud didn't make many of the Town Hall Concerts. This is why.

Backstage after a concert with Ernie Anderson (at left) admiring all the people he helped assemble

Brother can you spare a bass

Eddie Condon

"Creative Listening",
ROBERT A. SIMON IN
—THE NEW YORKER

"Rousing ... Vigorous
...A Wow",
WILDER HOBSON IN
—TIME

"Le Jazz Intellectuel"
EMILY COLEMAN IN
—NEWSWEEK

"A Stellar Program"
DAVID QUIRK IN
—THE DAILY NEWS

"Most absorbing musical
experience I have been
through",
VIRGIL THOMSON IN
—THE HERALD TRIBUNE

"Stirring"
HOWARD TAUBMAN IN
—THE NEW YORK TIMES

Presenting 30 of the
Greatest Living
Hot Musicians
October 16
MONDAY EVENING
8:40 P. M.

$1.00 to 2.50
(PLUS TAX)

at Carnegie Hall

JOHNNY DE VRIES'S POSTER FOR CARNEGIE HALL CONCERT

A view from the one-dollar seats

WAR DEPARTMENT

THE ARMED FORCES RADIO SERVICE

presents

PART 1   Prog. Time & Fill 30:00

EDDIE CONDON

This transcription is the property of the War Department of the United States Government and use for commercial purposes is prohibited.

THE ARMED FORCES RADIO SERVICE
TRANSCRIBED 48 OF OUR CONCERTS.

The second best vestibule business in town.

A small but determined group

In 1944 we began to do a scheduled radio show on the Blue Network. We broadcast at 1:30 EWT (Eastern War Time) on Saturdays but as the broadcasts continued we were shifted at some point to later in the afternoon. The half-hour show featured the men who played at my scheduled concerts at Town Hall or Carnegie Hall. We broadcast from either Town Hall or the Ritz Theater, which was actually a broadcast studio, and when they began sending our music, the transcribed version that is, overseas, the response was incredible.

Our shows were transcribed by the Armed Forces Radio Service and broadcast around the world to all the servicemen. We were happy to do our part at morale-boosting and we were lucky enough to win first place in the GI popularity poll. I don't know who all the competition was but we beat out Guy Lombardo and the Hit Parade. This was at a time when some people didn't think our music could be accepted at all, let alone even finish in a popularity poll. It was very satisfying.

We continued the broadcasts through 1947, when we went on to television. TV was great but our most spontaneous effort was on radio. We just had to come to a hall and play and the audience had a chance to listen.

Hot Mahatma

Eddie Condon's Jazz Concerts on the Blue Network give spontaneous American music its best airing

"THIS IS THE MOST MAGNIFICENT NOISE I HAVE HEARD SINCE THE FALL OF KRONSTADT," a Russian listener telegraphed from Washington after he had tuned in *Eddie Condon's Jazz Concert* one Saturday afternoon this summer. "I CONGRATULATE YOU WITH ALL MY EAR." Five weeks after its inception on May 20th, the half-hour broadcast of genuine hot music was drawing more than a thousand similar messages of congratulation a week—a greater response than any sustaining program had received since Bing Crosby made his air debut a decade ago. Though at the end of its initial 13-week series no commercial sponsor had been found, the network gave the program an indefinite extension. Continuing in effect will be the clause, probably unique in radio, that Condon insisted on including in the contract: "In order to preserve the unrestrained ad lib qualities of this music, the artists may depart from the formal program at any time."

Eddie's unrestrained guests include the finest jazz musicians within hailing distance of the studio—men like Edmond Hall, Gene Krupa, Hot Lips Page, Joe Marsala, Jonah Jones, Max Kaminsky, James P. Johnson, Muggsy Spanier. Regulars include Lee Wiley, whose sweetly husky voice goes beautifully with a hot background, and Peewee Russell, clarinetist extraordinary who plays with Eddie at Nick's in Greenwich Village—whenever Condon isn't in the process of being fired and rehired. Often criticised for his failure to take solos, Condon is unbeatable at the crisp, rhythmic four-string chording that sparks many jazz classics recorded under his name for Commodore and others.

PAGE 6   "PIC"

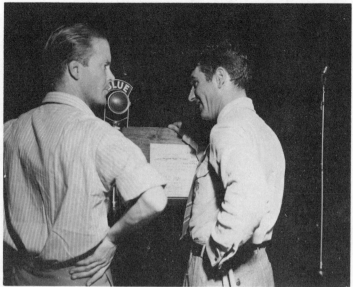

Gene Krupa was on as many broadcasts as possible; he was always welcome.

PLAYBACK OF A TRANSCRIPTION

Lee Wiley was the only female vocalist we ever used on the broadcasts. That's no mystery.

JONAH JONES

Noon	News, Clyde Kittell	Man on the Farm..	Jean Tighe, songs..	Theater of Today:
12:15	Consumer Time....	" "	Radie Harris.....	Janet Blair ....
12:30	Atlantic Spotlight:	News, H. Gladstone	News; Farm & Home	Hollywood Stars:
12:45	Trans-oceanic show	The Answer Man..	Harry Kogen Orch.	Guest ....
1:00	Saturday Rhythms:	Sen. Claude Pepper,	Eddie Condon's	Grand Central
1:15	Milton Katim Orch	Judge C. F. Collins	Jazz Concert....	Station; news..
1:30	The Baxters, drama	Symphonies for Youth	Soldiers With Wings	Report to the Nation:
1:45	War Telescope....	Alfred Wallenstein,	" "	John Daly......
2:00	These Are Our Men:	Los Angeles Phil-	Metropolitan opera:	Of Men and Books.
2:15	Staats Cotsworth	harmonic Orch.	Thomas' 'Mignon,'	Science Adventures
2:30	Musicana: Joseph	News, Leo Egan..	Rise Stevens,	Carolina Hayride:
2:45	Gallicchio's Orch	Stanley Maxted...	Mimi Benzell,	Southern folk music
3:00	Orchestras of Nation:	This Is Halloran:	James Melton,	The Land Is Bright:
3:15	Baltimore Sym-	Stan Lomax.....	Ezio Pinza,	Dramatization ..
3:30	phony Orchestra,	Where Are They Now	Donald Dame,	Syncopation Piece.
3:45	Reginald Stewart	Archdale Jones..	John Gurney	Job for Tomorrow.
4:00	Doctors Look Ahead	News, Leo Egan..	others; Wilfred	Washington Report
4:15	Dr. W. W. Bauer	John Richards Orch.	Pelletier,	Overseas Report ..
4:30	Music on Display:	Music for Half Hour	conductor	Assignment Home..
4:45	Clarence Fuhrman	Annette Burford.	" "	
5:00	Grand Hotel: Drama	Uncle Don........	" "	Philadelphia Orch.
5:15	Barbara Luddy..	Names in Action...	To be announced..	Eugene Ormandy,
5:30	John W. Vandercook	Bob Sherwood Orch	Hello, Sweetheart..	Edna Phillips,
5:45	Tin Pan Alley of Air	Shirley Eder......		harp soloist ....

Looking at this old schedule I see we were opposite a couple of politicians, the news, and a band I never heard of. No wonder our rating was good. We warmed up everyone for the Met.

"Joe, hide the music! Don't embarrass us!"

A BROADCAST FROM THE RITZ THEATER

Eddie Condon.

Concert Ends Jazz Season

Eddie Condon will give the last of the season's Jazz Concerts at Town Hall next Saturday afternoon. As a result of the success of the series a full schedule of concerts has been contracted for next season.

Three concerts under Mr. Condon's direction will be offered on weekday nights at Carnegie Hall. The first will be a joint recital with Duke Ellington and his orchestra, and John W. Bubbles, which is scheduled for October. In November a large list of jazz instrumentalists and singers will present The Jazz Music of George Gershwin. Louis Armstrong, performing with two small orchestras, a choir and Earl Hines, will appear at the third in this series.

The Town Hall recitals will begin Oct. 10 and continue on alternate Saturdays until May, 1943. Among the artists who will participate are Fats Waller, Louis Armstrong, Earl Hines, Benny Goodman, Bud Freeman, Jack Teagarden, Gene Krupa, Baby Dodds, Duke Ellington's entire orchestra and Count Basie and his orchestra.

Carnegie Can Take It

After some undergraduate work at Town Hall, Eddie Condon's jolly jazzmongers moved up to Carnegie Hall last night for some higher studies in swing and sweet.

With orchestra and soloists running through a sheaf of hot and not so hot numbers, Carnegie Hall took it soberly. After all, the hall has taken a lot, from Shostakovich fortissimos to Jack Benny's concert debut.

The program breezed through the whole wardrobe, from rag all the way down the line. Some 30 "hot" musicians worked the wonders, with Eddie doubling as guitarist and conductor-emcee.

Listed sections included solo and orchestral provisations, a tribute to Fats Waller, and a final jam session.

Among billed participants were James P. Johnson, Willie The Lion, Art Hodes, Max Kaminsky, Mugsy Spanier, Hot Lips Page, Benny Morton, Peewee Russell, Bob Haggart and vocalists Lee Wiley and Red McKenzie.

Condon Jazz Concert Here Wins Greater Ovation Than in Gotham

Eddie Condon's first Bridgeport jazz concert Wednesday night at the Lyric theater was acclaimed as an outstanding success by an appreciative audience which applauded, whistled, stamped its feet and shouted for more when jazzdom's famed "Barefoot Boy" and his troupe of 12 musicians had concluded a fast-moving evening with a rousing jam session.

The concert attracted not only jazz enthusiasts from Bridgeport and its surrounding towns, but also a group of hot music fans from New York and Waterbury. Among them was J. Robert Mantler, editor of the American Jazz Review, who expressed surprise over the enthusiastic applause which he said surpassed even that accorded the Condon concerts in New York's Town hall or Carnegie hall.

Audience Cheers

Saxophonist Bud Freeman's improvisations on "I Got Rhythm," with rhythm support by Joe Bushkin on piano, Sid Weiss, bass, and Johnny Blowers, drums, brought cheers from the audience. Pianist Joe Sullivan's performance of "Room with a View," "Sweet Lorraine" and his original "Little Rock Getaway," with "Baby" Dodds at the drums, drew an equally enthusiastic response.

An eight-piece combination opened the program, with Joe Thomas on trumpet; Johnny Mince, clarinet; Vernon Brown, trombone; Freeman, Bushkin, Weiss, Blowers, and Condon himself strumming guitar. Mince, Thomas, Freeman and Brown all provided inspired solos, particularly on "Sugar" and "Royal Garden Blues."

Most unusual feature of the concert was Dodds' drum specialty which demonstrated the famous New Orleans jazzman's virtuosity in various intricate styles of drumming. Other noteworthy solos were pianist Bushkin's original "Serenade in Thirds," trombonist Brown's "Black and Blue," trumpeter Thomas' "Talk of the Town," trombonist Fred Ohms' "I Surrender Dear," clarinetist Mince's "After I say I'm Sorry" and Freeman's "Indian Summer."

Max Kaminsky Scores Hit

Trumpeter Max Kaminsky scored a decided hit with an original "D. A. R. Blues," inspired by the Daughters' recent refusal to allow Condon to stage a jazz concert in Constitution hall. Kaminsky was joined by Ohms, Mince, Freeman, Bushkin, Blowers and Weiss in an inspired jam session performance of "The Sheik of Araby" to close the first half of the program.

When the curtain rose for the final jam session concluding the program, Dodds and Blowers were both seated at drums in center stage, and Sullivan and Bushkin were at pianos on each side of the stage. With Weiss strumming the bass, this stellar rhythm group established a blues pattern on which each musician improvised choruses as Condon called them on the stage one by one. After the 12 concert stars were all on stage, improvising collectively and singly, Condon hopped around pointing to one man after another, signaling for each to do a solo break.

When the lengthy applause subsided after the closing curtain, Condon expressed his gratitude to the audience and explained that the musicians "would like to play until tomorrow noon, or even until next Easter" but that they had to catch a train to New York. He added that they would gladly return to Bridgeport for another concert in the fall after their summer trip to Hollywood and a series of European concerts for which they have been signed.—W.R.C.

HEARD AND OVERHEARD

This Is Radio

From comedians' jokes to new shows the Big Four networks are frightened by imagination and nurse a stultifying fetish for the familiar. If it's new it won't do.

Eddie Condon

Most current and painful example of a major network's inability to fathom anything outside the prosaic mold is Blue's (what stroke of genius possessed them to drop that easy, well-established handle?) recent treatment of Eddie Condon's *Saturday Afternoon Jazz Concerts.*

Condon's free-wheeling, non-Jim Crow, weekly presentation of American music by a group of the most uninhibited, imaginative jazz musicians in the country played a shifting Saturday afternoon sustaining spot for over a year. It overcame almost blank listening hours and attracted a formidable following in North America and among the armed forces abroad. Its fan mail built up to a terrific weight but even this usually-desirable form of pressure wasn't enough to make an impression on the mighty skulls of Blue.

This Spring Condon was told to inject a comedian, jive talk (which he and his musicians don't understand), a gushy gal singer, and the other lemon rinds and cherries that go to make up the typical radio cocktail, into his musical program. Nuts, Eddie said, the show rides as is or you know what you can do with it. His vacancy is now being filled by something indescribable labeled *Saturday Afternoon Senior Prom.*

The pull of Condon's shows lay in their naturalness, their freedom from the phony. Condon and his artists refused to louse up their presentation with what passes for "showmanship" in the radio world. The announcer, Fred Robbins, was asked to talk like a human being and, by gosh, he did. Condon, during his turns at the microphone, said what he wanted to say without the dictates of office-prepared script. And the musicians played the tunes they thought best in the way they thought they should be played. Musical arrangements were not there to curb their conception, something that never failed to horrify the Blue's biggies.

The over-all result was highly satisfying to everyone—except the Blue. The Blue wanted Condon and his men to wear saddles. When band leaders such as Tommy and Jimmy Dorsey, Jack (Big T) Teagarden, Gene Krupa, Woody Herman and others came to town they were glad to sit in with Eddie's ensemble—and for the usual $24 that everyone else was paid for his half-hour of giving. This would indicate what the big musicians thought of the idea.

On his show Condon used, from time to time, such great Negro and white interpreters and executors of true jazz as Bobby Hackett, Peewee Russell, Jess Stacy, James J. Johnson, Gene Schroeder, Willie the Lion Smith, Muggsy Spanier, George Wettling, Max Kaminsky, Joe Marsala, Miff Mole, Billy Butterfield, Kansas Fields, Sid Bechet, Joe Bushkin, Bob Casey, Bob Hagert and so on for 10 or 15 other names out of the top drawer of jazz. Most of these musicians are not young men. Their names make up the history of jazz and they ARE jazz.

If one of the other major networks—or a sponsor not presently sponsoring—wanted to they could give Blue the laugh and profit by a large, ready-made, anxiously-waiting audience by reassembling the Condon group, letting it have its head and allowing barefoot music again to swell periodically throughout the land.

—J. S. QUALEY

(PM's Radio Editor, Edwin Levin, is on vacation.)

Eddie's Guest

Ray McKinley, whose new band is now at the Commodore Hotel, plays a special drums medley with this afternoon's jazz concert at Town Hall. The concert is under the inimitable, exacting, sensitive and flowerlike baton of somebody named Eddie Condon.

CONCERTS

The Sweetheart of the D. A. R.

Eddie Condon

Now in his 5th concert season will present a typical Americondon group of famous jazz artists at Town Hall.

THIS AFTERNOON AT 5:30

Hot Jazz Concert Given at Academy of Music

Hot jazz rode with a solid beat into the Academy of Music last night, and the floorboards are still throbbing.

From the opening moment of the Eddie Condon Jazz Concert, when Max Kaminsky pointed his battered trumpet at the chandelier and the ensemble tore into "I Found a New Baby," the near capacity audience found the music hot and to its liking.

It was music for those who take their jazz seriously — the straight Dixieland of "Ballin' the Jack" and "Jazz Me Blues," the Chicago boogie of Pinetop Smith, and the Harlem party piano of "Honeysuckle Rose."

Stage arrangements were appropriately informal. The musicians, top flight jazz men, wandered on or off the stage as needed. But whether the ensemble was large or small, the free improvisation which is the soul of jazz always was present.

There was masterful solo work — terrific riffs on the wild cornet of Muggsy Spanier, intricate work on the big bass by Bob Haggart, and sound clarinet passages by Joe Dixon. The venerable James P. Johnson's piano was as effortless as ever, and the one local boy, Sam Price, drew a big hand with two examples of boogie woogie.

But the ensemble work was even more notable. In such items as the violently-paced "That's a Plenty," the group reached the free-swinging "ride" style of old time jazz. And in the jam session that marked the finale, even the explosive drum work of big clowning Sidney Catlett and Kansas Fields did not blast the music out of comprehensible bounds.

Much of the credit for the difficult task of stopping the improvisation from roaring into cacophony belongs to Mr. Condon. Dropping his guitar early in the evening, he wandered about the stage, commanding one instrument to come out, or another to quiet down. It was more conducting than usual for a jazz group, but the results were very agreeable.

There were several offerings by the slightly too sweet trumpet of Billy Butterfield, and a song interlude, pleasant but out of place, featuring blonde Lee Wiley.

It should also be mentioned that aside from much foot tapping on the red carpets, and one or two outbursts of rhythmic hand-clapping, the audience was free of jitterbug mannerisms. Hot jazz, you know, is a very serious thing.—F. McB.

Dear Mr. Condon,

I am thirteen years old and i listen to your broadcast every saturday afternoon...my mother wants me to go out and peddle flesh on Harney st because thats when all them sojers come in from Lincoln Nebraska and she thinks I can hustle a few bucks for the sunday roast... well, ma works over to the bomber plant on Saturdays so i get a chance to hear that real jazz and Mr. Condon, believe me, I'm in a real rut I get so groovey over it...the last groove I got into was when Stan Kenton was to the Orpheum and I really ain't got over it yet..and along comes your jive and I'm p ractically in a slit trench..Mr. Condon, believe me, I think you and your musicians is solid..now Mr. Condon, believe me, here's what I want to know...Me and some of the kids from Central is forming a Eddie Condon Hot club and we wondered if you got pins for this kind of organiz- ation..something we could all wear to show we 're Eddie Condon fans..if you has'nt made these up yet maybe you could send us a pixture of you and them musicians...I often wonder what Pee Wee Russell looks like...believe me, Mr. Condon I go for his kind of playing...that Hackett is strictly too Mr. Condon and I hope you go far with this new kind of music...E lsie Burton, a girlfriend I hang out with likes the bush and I'm trying to intra duce her to this kind of knocked out jazz...with two sticks in her lungs and hearing your music I'm sure she would get sent out of this universe... maybe next Saturday you could dedicate one of these numbers to Elsie..she'd never get over it, believe me, Mr. Condon. Maybe you should like to know what I look like so I am enclosing a pixture of me which was taken at the lake last summer...I filled out since then, believe me, Mr. Condon and I ain't so bony.. I got small ankles and wrists and my hair when I tint it is bright red...maybe you go for this kind of chick, Mr. Condon...Is you married, by the way? I got such a jolt when after two years of listening to Frankie and I find out he's got a wife and kid..it makes a lot of difference, believe me, Mr. Condon..well, like I say if you could send us a pixture and maybe your life story or something we could start this here club and get the member- ship increased...Opal, thats another one of my girl friends here say she is coming to New York to get a job and will look you up when she gets in town... she thinks maybe she can get something in the Powers model office but I tell Opal its cold potatoes because Opal got to wear xelastic stockings..well, Mr. Condon...there's no use my running off to the mouth with this drivel and I know maybe your manager will tear it up and you'll never see it but anyway I got it offen my chest and believe me, Mr. Condon, when I say you made a little shut-ins life a little brighter...I got to duck nxxx this letter now... if my old lady catches me sitting here and not out trafficking she'll wallop my backsid e....

                         your fond admirer,

                         Muriel Holsumbake
                         2214 Cherry Avenue
                         Council Bluffs
                         Iowa.

Third Street and Points North

Burgess Meredith first put the idea of opening my own club in my mind. It rattled around in there for some time before I really had the slightest thought of doing it, but one night Nick told us he was raising the price of musicians' drinks from twenty-five to thirty cents. There was a place thirty yards from Nick's, also on Tenth Street, called Julius's, mainly patronized by seamen and dockworkers. When we weren't visiting friends at intermission at Nick's we would dash across the street to Julius's and sometimes take a few of Nick's customers (friends of ours) along.

There was a fellow named Pete Pesci who was manager of Julius's. Due to my various jazz concerts and recordings our kind of music had become more and more popular. After considerable deliberation Pete and I decided to open Eddie Condon's, at 47 West Third Street. The idea to open a club was the easiest part but after a lot of preparatory work, such as Russell Patterson's decorations, we opened in December 1945. The people never stopped coming until the owners of the building gave us and all our neighbors two years' notice and the whole area was turned into a gigantic housing project.

Pete and I both wanted to have the club to remain in the Village. My theory has always been "the closer my bed to the bandstand the better." I had lived in the Village since I opened at Nick's and Pete lived in an apartment over Julius's. At the time I lived in an apartment on Washington Square North recently vacated by Amy Vanderbilt, the "deanette" of etiquette. Our finding the apartment was a sort of miracle, because at that time apartments were as available as free gold mines. Phyllis's sister, Alberta, overheard two girls on a train from Washington discussing their boss, Amy Vanderbilt. Alberta asked how Amy Vanderbilt could be reached and was told her business number in the Empire State Building. She told us we could look at the apartment after business hours of the same day. That was a Monday (at that time we were nearby on West Twelfth). We moved in Friday of the same week. The reason for moving was that our second daughter, Liza, was expected in October and we needed larger quarters. We have been there ever since. It was a three-minute walk to work and sometimes it took one hundred and three to reel back.

Around the turn of the century the building that became the saloon was known as the Greenwich Village Mill. It was described as one block north from the Bleecker Street Sixth Avenue elevated station, one block south from the Fifth Avenue bus line terminus and a five-minute walk from the Ninth Street Hudson Tube station. We found this old postcard in the basement one day when Wild Bill and Gene Schroeder were building a model HO railroad. As the years went by the railroad became bigger and bigger and the breaks in the basement became longer and longer. The building must have been around forever; it looks like it says 1827 on the side. Just before we went in the building housed a joint called the Howdy Club featuring an all-boy, part-girl cast—an enormous cosmetic account.

Inside the place on opening night. The band was as the flyer indicated, itself a major accomplishment. Everyone on the stand seems to be playing: Brad on valve trombone, Wild Bill, Bud, Joe Marsala, Bob Casey, Gene Schroeder, and WOR on microphone. Dave Tough was the drummer and if you look carefully you can see a reflection of George Wettling in one of the mirrors. Most of the audience is unidentifiable, but Art Hodes is sitting next to Wettling's reflection, Weegee is holding the camera, Mrs. Joe Bushkin is next to the flashbulb, and Mr. and Mrs. Misha Reznikoff are the closest spectators to Brad's feet. The group pictured here was not a regular band and there was a new bunch in about two sets.

MUSIC

A Club of His Own

Eddie Condon once tried to tell a New York *Daily News*man, in the plainest language he could muster, about his troubles in making the "real jazz" pay enough for tea for two, or keep body & soul together night & day: "We bled to death. We were eating off each other's wrists. We had one paper hat right on the hook but when we mentioned money he jumped back in the icebox." Another potential sponsor died during negotiations: "He went cool on us. They had to throw dirt on him."

Last week, in spite of all, Guitarist Eddie Condon got a nightclub of his own,

doesn't play as much as he used to, now that he's a bandleader, but he has been around when some of the best jazz has been played. Condon acts as mother hen to as undependable a brood of gifted musicians as James Petrillo has in his roster. Eddie got them together first at Town Hall jazz concerts. They seemed willing to follow him—even when they couldn't follow everything he said, in his elliptical, corner-of-the-mouth mutter. Boasts Eddie: "There's not a blood relative in the band. . . . No red beards. The boys can dress as they please as long as they have shoes on."

Most conspicuous absentees at Eddie

among fellow players, follow Condon's own habits: boilermakers (whiskey with a beer chaser) at the bar and milk at home (he thinks milk will keep away ulcers).

Though he sometimes slips into their highfalutin language, Jazzman Condon scorns the earnest critics of jazz—and once earned the gratitude of his colleagues by his cavalier attitude toward a French expert on *le jazz hot*. Said Eddie: "I wouldn't think of going over there and telling them how to jump on a grape."

Command Performance

The rococo Paris Opera House last week had its first command performance for troops since Hitler and friends were entertained there in June 1940. This time the audience was a khaki blend of 2,200 G.I.s, WACs, British Tommies. They got

Lofman-Pix

EDDIE CONDON & BAND (OPENING NIGHT AT THE CLUB)
The boys were willing to follow what they didn't always understand.

where for the first time he was "eligible on both sides of the bar." Eddie Condon's, an incongruously plush spot, opened its doors in Manhattan's Greenwich Village and let out some of the loudest and longest renditions of *Tea for Two* and *I've Found a New Baby* to be heard since Prohibition.

Mother Hen to Jazz. There were good men on the bandstand: Saxman Bud Freeman; cocky, stocky Trumpeter Wild Bill Davison, who blows the horn out of the side of his mouth; zoot-suitish Clarinetist Joe (*Little Sir Echo*) Marsala, Drummers Dave Tough and George Wettling—all members of ragtime's Valhalla (Chicago branch) who have kept on playing jazz the old way, even after their pal Benny Goodman called it swing and made it a million dollar baby. There were no music stands or orchestrations to be seen at Eddie Condon's. "That's for organized slop," Eddie said.

Condon's men worked until 4 a.m. Sometimes Condon sat in, picking solemnly and matter-of-factly at his guitar. He

Condon's opening were some of Condon's fellow Chicagoans: Trombonist Milfred ("Miff") Mole, Cornetist Francis Xavier ("Muggsy") Spanier, who play a half mile away, at Nick's in the Village—where Condon played until about two years ago. (Twelve blocks away, Manhattanites could hear the far more virile and exciting New Orleans Negro jazz of Cornetist Bunk Johnson—TIME, Nov. 5.) Some of Nick's parishioners were scattered among Condon's opening-night audience, lost among the celebrities and the Hoosiers. "You know, Hoosiers," explained Condon, himself the ninth child of an Indiana saloonkeeper: "the Paramount-once-a-week, glass-top-bus crowd. They stick around hoping to get into a picture. I don't mind the Hoosiers. They can come down, sit down, shut up, drink and get charged."

Condon calls his new jazz temple "Town Hall with booze." ("Our music stimulates drinking. They figure in order to understand it, they got to do like the fellow playing it.") Few people, even

a lecture-demonstration of the mysteries of ballet.

The producers weren't sure just how much ballet G.I.s could stand, so they corned it up. The show traced the growth of a dancer from an eight-year-old student "rat" to the *première danseuse* in *Giselle*. Late in the evening, for the first time in its history, the Opera lifted all its backdrops, baring the entire 185-ft.-deep stage. Even members of the orchestra stood up in the pit to watch. Then stagehands in new blue uniforms (they refused to appear before the Americans in faded ones) changed sets, set up scenery for *Les Deux Pigeons* in two minutes, 30 seconds. In the lobby at intermission G.I.s talked knowingly of *entrechats*, and of how Nijinsky must have looked as Albrecht in *Giselle*. A U.S. newsman, hoping to send home a breezy story about mugs on a night out, stopped 100 soldiers, asked them if this was the first ballet they had ever seen. The condescending reply of G.I. balletomanes: "Are you kiddin'?"

RUSSELL PATTERSON AND DICK WALTERS, WHO HAVE JUST STEPPED AWAY FROM ONE OF THEIR MOST SUCCESSFUL NIGHT CLUB DESIGNS, REPORT THAT THE OPENING WILL BE **THURSDAY, DECEMBER 20TH.** A NEW STEINWAY GRAND HAS JUST ARRIVED FOR **JOE SULLIVAN,** OUR SOLOIST. **GENE SCHROEDER** WILL PLAY IT IN OUR AMERICONDON ORCHESTRA. **DAVE TOUGH**'s DRUMS, **BOB CASEY**'s BASS, **WILD BILL DAVISON**'s TRUMPET, **JOE MARSALA**'s CLARINET, & **BRAD GOWAN**'s VALVE TROMBONE, ARE ALL HERE AND UNCRATED. **BUD FREEMAN** HAS CHECKED IN WITH AN 18-KARAT MONDAY NIGHT JAZZ CONCERT ENSEMBLE. **THE MUTUAL NETWORK** HAS ITS MICROPHONES SET UP FOR A NEW COAST-TO-COAST **EDDIE CONDON** SERIES. **PETE PESCI** IS AT THE PHONE WAITING FOR YOUR RESERVATION (**GR 3-8736**). **EDDIE CONDON'S,** 47 WEST THIRD STREET, NEW YORK CITY 12. OPEN EVERY EVENING, 7:30 P. M. TO 4:00 A. M. **NO CONFETTI.**

Someone asked me in early December when we were going to open the place. I said we would open when the paint was dry. It dried by December 20 and we sent out fliers to prove it.

Tim Costello at the place on a busy night. He had his own bar at Third Avenue and Forty-Fourth Street. We had photographs on our walls; there were Thurber drawings all over Tim's. He used to stop by our place occasionally.

The saloon on West Third was the first place in the world with a jazz musician's name above the door. Paul Smith designed the sign and it became a symbol associated with me ever since. Red McKenzie coined the name porkchop at the Stork Club and later he shrunk the name to simply chop. We had vegetarians in the band and didn't want to offend anyone so he kept saying, "Where's the chop, where's the chop . . ." The name and Paul's symbolic design fit. It was a cold December in 1945, lots of snow and nobody on the street. Everyone was inside. This picture captures the club in a nice way, twenty-five years ago.

Which one is the doorman?

Big Fitz kept us honest at Third Street, but we always closed on time.

After opening night we settled down with our customary seven-piece band.

Closeup of the same band, same night. Tony is smiling because his hair is still in place. Wild Bill is sleeping, but hadn't missed a note for the whole first set. Dave looks as though he is reading War and Peace *on his tomtom, and Jack is taking the solo.*

(Left) Once upon a time there was a book and later a movie called Young Man With A Horn. It was one of Grimm's fairy tales. Bix is still revolving in his grave over the book and if he had been alive when the movie came out he wouldn't have lasted long. Anyway, Kirk Douglas was going to play the lead in the movie and he came down to the club to get the "atmosphere of jazz" and to learn how to hold a cornet. He was a fine guy and caught on fast. Sidney Bechet is helping here and Art Hodes looks casual. Pee Wee is auditioning for a drink.

Kirk with the full band: Georg Brunis, Peanuts Hucko, Gene Schroeder, Buddy Rich, and Jack Lesberg. In dead center, the polished area was the original rink design for Ice Capades of 1952.

Bogeaus and Meredith Mull Jazz Pic on Eddie Condon

Story of modern jazz has been set as the next venture of the indie production team of Benedict Bogeaus and Burgess Meredith. Tentatively titled as "The Life of Eddie Condon," film's lead will be played by Jimmy Stewart with screenplay by novelist John O'Hara.

Meredith met Condon a few years back when former was due to play Bix Biederbecke in Vinton Freedley's projected legit production of "Young Man With a Horn." Play never was put on because of script trouble but may yet be filmed.

Two great songwriters. Johnny Mercer and Willard Robison. John's wife Ginger is on the right. I first got to know Willard at the Markwell Hotel where he played piano in the bar. A lot of musicians stayed there and when they sometimes fell behind in their rent they locked up their baggage; the place was commonly called the trunk store. Willard played a beat-up piano in the bar and probably wrote some of his best songs there. Nobody has ever said much about him but nobody wrote prettier songs. Willard died a couple of years ago and Pee Wee, Jack Palmer, Lee Wiley, and I went to his wake. We were all alone.

Rex must not have been paying attention to my suit. I wish I still had it; it would be right back in style. Rex was never out of style even after he stopped playing and moved to Albany. In later years he had a radio show and started writing. It's too bad he never put his whole story together. With his talent and adventures it would have been a winner.

Bob Mitchum likes jazz. He used to come in all the time when he was in town.

The Duke and Duchess of Windsor. Mrs. William O'Dwyer (Sloan Simpson) brought them by. They seemed to have a good time but judging by the way the Duke hummed along with some of the tunes I'm not surprised he didn't last as king. Anyway, he was a helluva nice guy.

Cutty Cutshall, Ruby Braff, and Herb Hall. Leonard Gaskins is in the background. Herb is still carrying on the tradition of his brother Edmund: both played Albert-system clarinets, but Herb also plays tenor. Ruby has a facility for turning down work but always has expensive cars. I don't think he is a car thief because he never leaves his house. He's a particular guy, though, when it comes to what and where he plays. Tony Bennett carries two guys on the road with him. One of them is Ruby.

Somebody has written on this picture that it is the JV band. If this is the scrub team I'd hate to see the regulars. In fact this is the band that played at the club while I was in England on tour in 1957. Johnny Varro is the pianist and Arvell Shaw is on bass. This must have been one of the few times that Arvell was not on the road with Louis Armstrong. He played with him during the fifties and sixties.

Vic Dickenson didn't start playing at the club until well into the fifties. I got together with him for an extended period a few years later during a far eastern tour. This picture was taken on a Tuesday night, ham session night, when we added two guys to the regular crew. Over the years I have gotten to know him better and even got to introduce him every so often when he was recording at the Roosevelt Grill in 1970. The chins in the background belong to Jim McPartland.

We always had a pianist alternate with the band at Third Street. Joe Sullivan was there as often as anyone. Here he is playing a duet with Dick Wellstood, who is so young he is probably wearing knickers. While Dick was a law student he used to run around with a card that said, "My name's Dick Wellstood. Can you help me meet Joe Sullivan?" Somebody helped him here.

(Left) This is as close to a regular band at the club as you can probably come, except that George Wettling was there more than Buzzy Drootin. You note that I am keeping my eyes on the audience. This may have been the night that Henry Fonda was in the place and John Huston was as well. Henry didn't know John was there and John borrowed one of the waiters' red- and-white jackets and went up to wait on Henry's table. Henry didn't pay too much attention until John purposely spilled a drink on him. Henry didn't recognize John until he was soaked. Cutty, Wild Bill, Edmund, Gene, Buzzy, and probably Jack Lesberg are in the band.

We are probably talking about "Jamboree Jones." Johnny wrote it and Bing sang it.

I gave Johnny Windhurst the first steady job he had in his life. This may well be during his first run at the club. He is in there with the pros and he cut it pretty well, even though everyone has their eyes closed. It looks like a pretty sleepy band.

Dream Street Beat:
A Club That Hopes You'll Go Home

It was a typically quiet night at Eddie Condon's jazz emporium in Greenwich Village. The waiters were tired and wanted to go home. The bar was closed and the cash regis-

Eddie Condon (right) and his boys make music seriously.

ter locked. All doors were bolted. The customers had all gone home. But still nobody could get Hot Lips Page and his cornet off the bandstand.

The rest of the mob was up there, too, playing just for each other and, as usual, playing just a little better than they ever played for the customers. There was no way to get the lads out of the joint except throw them out. After a while the manager, Pete Pesci, did so.

Condon's has been in operation for almost six years, a longish period for any kind of night club,

and dealing as it does with jazz musicians it has furnished jazz buffs like this one with many a whacky memory. It was here, not long ago, that composer Bernie Hannighen told the details of his visit to Philadelphia with pianist Joe Bushkin. It seems Bernie and Joe were walking past Independence Hall when the great, cracked Liberty Bell fell out of its belfry and landed on the sidewalk right behind them.

"What's that?" demanded the startled Hannighen.

"That's F Sharp," Joe told him without even looking around.

Over the years, the Condon bands have had some rare characters. There was one musician who could not be fired because he was regularly five weeks ahead of himself in the salary department. This affected his disposition.

"He never disappoints us," Condon used to explain. "Either he's sober and won't play right or he's drunk and can't play right. He's the most dependable man I have."

There has been only one real tough spot in the Condon club history. It almost went under the first Summer it operated.

"They almost sent the police," he relates. "In fact, they did try to arrest us by mail."

Last Winter the Condon mob got

a little bored with each other (they've been bored with the customers for years) and decided they needed a hobby. The hobby they agreed upon was the operation of toy trains in the basement. They chipped in, bought trains, switches, gimmicks and several miles of miniature tracks. For some weeks the Condon kitchen couldn't bake anything because the miniature railroad was using the bake oven for a tunnel.

Artistically, Eddie is possibly best remembered for his analysis of foreign critics of jazz. One Hugues Panassie is a world-famed French authority on jazz, and although he is a fan of Condon's music, Eddie is unimpressed with French critics.

"After all," he explains, "I wouldn't have the gall to go over there and tell them how to jump on a grape."

Automobiles fascinate musicians the way diamonds intrigue a gentleman-preferred blonde. Bill Davison, Eddie's veteran cornetist, is

perhaps the busiest automobile collector. Bill once bought a station wagon (on time), sold it to another musician (on time), bought a Cadillac (on time) most sold the Cadillac (ditto) to buy a bopper and better station wagon (also ditto). This simple transaction is believed to have sent the presidents of two separate finance companies to mental hospitals.

Never an advocate of the solid foods, Eddie has long since known what to do about hangovers and, years ago, he gave to the world his unfailing recipe for a hangover cure. It's simple.

"Take the juice of two quarts of whisky," he advises.

Anytime Yul was in New York City he was a cinch to drop by. We were good friends.

Opening night. The best vestibule business in town. Joe Bushkin, Min Pious, Johnny DeVries (center) and Clark Jones.

PETE PESCI AT JULIUS'S

Eddy Gilmore with Wild Bill and Gene Schroeder. Eddy was with the Associated Press and once wrote a short piece about me.

New York Journal-American   –Tues., March 9, 1954

Master of Jazz And Articulation

By EDDY GILMORE

ONE of the most articulate men in America is a banjo player who never got beyond the eighth grade. His name is Eddie Condon (born Albert Edward Condon), a high priest of pure jazz, who has a consistency akin to the late Babe Ruth's.

The Babe never threw to a wrong base. Eddie never played a wrong chord.

After an honest start on the banjo, Condon has come down to the guitar and he's one of the best in the business. He's a man not given to bragging. The only self-praise I ever heard him indulge in was the remark, "I've never played a solo in my life."

It's Eddie's articulation with words, not music, that fascinates so many of his listeners and friends. Consider his comment on an eminent French music critic who denounced Americ'n jazz.

"Who does that Frog think he is," asked Eddie, "to come over here and try to tell us how to play? We don't go over there and tell them how to jump on a grape."

That is typical of Eddie.

No Opinion on Bop

Condon has no opinion on the subject of bop. He just never thinks of it. If he did I'm sure he would loathe it, but someone played a bop record for him the other day and insisted that he comment.

"I sat through a hurricane in 1944 on a beach out in Jersey," said Eddie, "and this is very reminiful of it."

"Perhaps," observed the man who was interviewing him, "but how do you rate the record?"

"How do you rate a hurricane?" asked Eddie.

Condon's observations on the human scene and on human beings are not confined to musicians. He introduced me to a college professor one night and later told me the prof once played football for Notre Dame.

"He looks a little old and frail for that," I said.

"Oh, he was playing before they put air in the football," he said.

The Condon household in New York's Greenwich Village is a seven-room contradiction.

It's the apartment of a musician, yet there isn't a guitar or a banjo in the place.

Condon has made at least 500 phonograph records in his life, but there's no phonograph in his apartment and not a single record.

Eddie appreciates Scotch whisky, but not on the home grounds. No bottle ever appears in the place unless some friends bring it. Down at his night club, however, Mr. Condon is known as a free pourer.

Hangover Remedy

He has an unusual remedy for hangovers.

"For a hangover," he suggests, "take the juice of two quarts of whisky."

Actually, he drinks 20 times as much milk as he does strong spirit. He eats nothing during the daylight hours, but his liquid par is three quarts of sweet milk and one quart of buttermilk.

His friend and cornet player, Wild Bill Davison recently opened an antiques shop somewhere on the Hudson.

"What are you going to call it?" Eddie asked.

"Trash and Treasures," said Bill.

Eddie shook his head.

"What's wrong with that name?"

"Nothing," said Eddie, "but I would have called it 'Wild Bull and His China Closet.'"

Condon is the sort of friend who doesn't give you one key to his apartment. He gives you several.

"Tomorrow," he said to me one day, "when you're out in the world, will you have some keys made to this place?"

"How many?"

"One for Phyllis (his clever, pretty wife), one for me, one for the maid and four for you," he said. "You lose things."

An after-hours jam session. In addition to the regulars, Gerry Mulligan, Bobby Brookmeyer, and Don Elliott have joined in to entertain Billy Holiday and Françoise Sagan.

CUTTY

WITH RITA HAYWORTH AND ESCORT

Davey Tough in action

JOE BUSHKIN, AVIS ASHCRAFT, EDDIE, PEANUTS HUCKO

Lee Wiley and Bix imitators

In 1958 our two years' notice expired at Third Street. I didn't think it was time to stop running a club so Pete Pesci and I started hunting around for other quarters.

Eddie Condon Back at Old Stand

Guitarist Is Leading Group Again After Lapse of a Year

By JOHN S. WILSON

EDDIE CONDON, the garrulous guitarist whose duties as host at his club, Condon's, 330 East Fifty-sixth Street, have often kept him so busy conversing with the customers that his guitar has remained untouched for nights on end, has put himself back on full time duty as a musician.

For the first time in more than a year, the band at Condon's is under Mr. Condon's leadership and he is celebrating the occasion by mounting the stand for every set, giving the downbeat for fast numbers with several reckless raps on the shell of his guitar and starting the slower ones with commanding thumps of his heel.

The group that Mr. Condon has assembled has a front line that represents three generations of jazz. Pee Wee Russell, the clarinetist looking more than ever like an embarrassed Thurber hound, has been playing off and on with Mr. Condon for more than thirty years; Marshall Brown, valve trombonist, began his professional career as a guitarist in pre-war swing bands; while Ruby Braff, cornetist, a slight, raffish elf over whom both Mr. Brown and Mr. Russell tower, is a post-war musician with well developed pre-war roots. With Mr. Condon in the rhythm section are Jack Keller, piano, and Ronnie Bedford, drums.

Organized Youth Band

This is the first time that Mr. Brown has appeared in New York as a small-group trombonist. He is best known as the organizer and leader of the Newport Youth Band, which was created three years ago by the Newport Jazz Festival, and before that as the developer of a high school band at Farmingdale, L. I., which was so accomplished that it was invited to appear at Newport, where it had an outstanding success.

Since the riot at Newport last summer put the Youth Band's sponsor out of business, Mr. Brown has been

Eddie Condon is playing regularly at his club, Condon's

making plans for a sextet of which he is joint leader with Mr. Braff. The sextet is already a reality but regular engagements for it are not, and while they are waiting to fulfill a four-week booking in Toronto in September, Mr. Brown and Mr. Braff have welcomed the opportunity to join Mr. Condon's group.

Although the Brown-Braff Sextet will play tightly written arrangements in what Mr. Brown describes as "a sort of Kansas City Seven-John Kirby-Gerry Mulligan Sextet style," the arrangements at Condon's are, as usual, nonexistent. The repertory leans toward mellowly propulsive treatments of such soundly melodic popular tunes as "Mean to Me," "As Long As I Live," "I'm Yours" and "Birth of the Blues."

Cornetist Without Peer

The Dixieland warhorses are trotted out occasionally to placate out-of-town visitors but these musicians are reluctant Dixielanders and they manage to coat these normally staccato tunes with a smoothly swinging veneer.

Mr. Braff is an unusually rewarding cornetist. He is now almost without a peer as an exponent of richly melodic jazz. His soft, low-register solos, his manner of slithering slyly from note to note and the brilliance of his biting attack when he moves into the upper register give his playing a constant sense of excitment.

Mr. Russell has distilled his uniquely cryptic musical shorthand to a feathery fineness, turning his solos into a series of light and lovely cameos. A balance for both men is provided by Mr. Brown whose valve trombone manages to be both gruff and flowing, somewhat reminiscent of the playing of the late Brad Gowans.

As for Mr. Condon, he is, as ever, a thoroughly unobtrusive guitarist, sitting off at one side of the stand, strumming industriously and displaying what one enthusiast the other evening kept insisting was "the greatest left hand in the business."

Eddie Condon's Move Gives Bob the Blues

By ROBERT C. RUARK.

LONDON, Feb. 5.—I am informed that Mr. Edwardo Condon, possibly for cause, has been ejected from his smoky cavern in New York's Greenwich Village and is now assaulting the midnight air from the elite East Side. I hope he'll be happy there, but I doubt it.

Robert C. Ruark

Mr. Condon, a professional minstrel who specializes in jazz and is also a sort of bum like me, has been removed from his cave because New York University gobbled up all the real estate in Eddie's sector of the Village. I think this is wrong. Did they get the Mills Hotel as well? It seems to me that tearing down the el and making a boulevard of Sixth Ave. has started an unhealthy trend.

I wish to come forth firmly as an avowed enemy of all progress. I would gladly give up the airplane and the auto if it put the buggywhip factories back to work. I would abjure penicillin if it raised the market value of sulphur and molasses.

* * *

Nor do I like the way they are monkeying around with jazz, and especially the old-timey advocates like Condon. Very seriously, a pink-cheeked English lass inquired the other day as to which school of jazz moderne I was affiliated, and I couldn't answer.

I don't care about all the cultured approaches to jazz, where it is reviewed and analyzed and plucked apart, and called progressive or decadent or San Francisco versus New Orleans. I say, leave it alone and let the people pound and toot and strum and enjoy the noise.

Jelly Roll Morton, bless his departed soul, was one of the fathers of the art as we know it, and he raised me in a loft on U St. in Washington after he left N_Awlins and Chicago. The great man would have been out of place in an air-conditioned palace full of chrome and fine feathers.

Jazz needs a simulation of a murky New Orleans midnight or a low dive in Chicago. It calls for dim lights and lousy service and a bunch of worthless people to make it jump, because jazz is about half audience participation anyhow.

It is a strange thing, but when you uproot an art form from its habitat something undefinable happens to the mood. I cite you the bistro of Joe and Tim Costello, where all the writing people used to hang out. It only moved one door away, and the same folks still drink and eat there, but it has never really been the same.

I hope that this doesn't happen to Mr. Condon, that persuasive gentleman who is a better writer than he ever was a guitar player, and who speaks a prose that can only be described as architecturally modern. He called me once and said, quote: "Meet me at the numerical place at the rich man's dawn, and we will have our psyches halfsoled."

This I translated correctly as "Meet me at the 21 club at 6 p.m. and we'll have a drink."

I sincerely hope that progress will not get in the way of gut-bucket blues, and that the tootlers and thumbers won't go uptown on me just because they got a fresh location. This has happened before when you take the boys out of the boondocks and introduce them to shoes.

We moved the pictures to the bandstand when we decorated the uptown saloon. Maxie's the only trumpet player I know who uses the drum as a mutestand. Red Richards on piano, with Vic Dickenson and Bob Wilber.

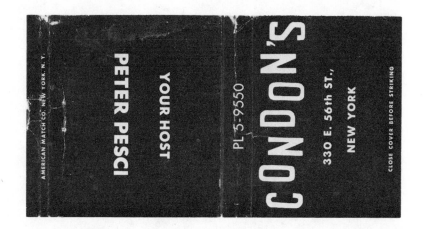

AMERICAN MATCH CO. NEW YORK, N.Y.

PETER PESCI

YOUR HOST

PL 5-9550

CONDON'S

330 E. 56th ST., NEW YORK

CLOSE COVER BEFORE STRIKING

Some of my best friends were less than enthusiastic about the move.

Stanley Kubrick used to take still photos before he got into movies. He took this one at the club one night.

"*Did you know Eddie Condon's is open for dinner and cocktails at 5 P.M.?*"

Ham Fisher liked jazz. I gave a copy of this sketch to my tailor. I also gave a copy to Gibson and they sent me a banjo with no strings.

TV

I accidentally had the first jazz concert on television, in April 1942. It was an accident because a CBS executive, Worthington Minor, had just happened by one of my Town Hall concerts. He liked what he saw and we broadcast four shows before Federal Communications Commission wartime restrictions shut us down, along with almost everyone else. It was no loss; there were probably about three people watching us on three-inch screens.

It was a few years before I got a regular show on WPIX. After a year on WPIX they failed to pick up the option on my show. I'm glad they didn't because Bob Sarnoff did and we had a happy and extensive run on Saturday nights on NBC. NBC and a few other people liked us but we scared potential sponsors to death. No one would touch us with a barge pole, but we managed to hold out unsponsored. I'm sure there were some products we could have moved on TV but they still don't allow things like that to be advertised.

The Eddie Condon Floorshow, as it was called, was just a group of guys playing with some added attractions such as singers and dancers and musical sketches.

Jack is wearing the judge's robes. This is where we first played the song Sidney Smith and I put together, called "We Called It Music," about the time of the book. Jack starts off by saying "Order in the courtroom . . ." and this is a little number we worked up for the song.

We played a tribute to W. C. Handy one night. He was in the studio and at one point he slowly started tapping his foot as we played one of his songs. We were proud.

Ernie Anderson. He was everywhere during the TV series.

Misha Reznikoff came in and improvised some sketches on some of the shows.

BOBBY HACKETT

Maggie always liked TV shows. Now she helps produce them. With Artie Shaw and Elvis Presley.

Zutty, Jack, and Porkchop

I wonder if that box was on camera.

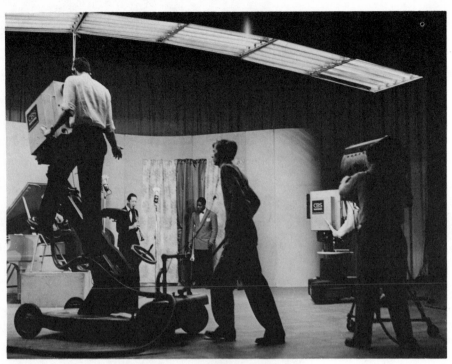

ZUTTY SINGLETON, LIPS PAGES, JAMES P. JOHNSON

EDDIE, JACK LESBERG, BUDDY RICH

Jam session

Roy Eldridge and a hot trumpet

Condon, Ella Fitzgerald, Sid Bechet

The maestro and Gene Krupa

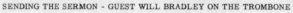

SENDING THE SERMON - GUEST WILL BRADLEY ON THE TROMBONE

I had heard of Doc Souchon but never met him until this moment on This Is Your Life. *It was his life so I wasn't going to complain; I didn't know Ralph Edwards either. Doc was a banjo player and raconteur from New Orleans who delivered well over 10,000 babies in his lifetime. He knew more about New Orleans music than any three critics you could think of put together.*

W.COTTON

Making Records

Milt Gabler's Commodore sessions kept us all in business. There were Commodore sessions built around Bud Freeman, the Kansas City Five and Six, Chu Berry, Jess Stacy, Willie the Lion Smith, Billie Holiday, Joe Sullivan, and sometimes Eddie Condon and his Band. There were no bad Commodore records and the line-ups here show why.

This was the first Commodore record and it was also the first twelve-inch record of real improvised jazz. Thank you, Mr. Gabler. We did it the day after Benny Goodman's concert in Carnegie Hall in 1938 and that accounts for the titles of the tunes. The records were an artistic success and it sold a few copies. I think we made a little history.

"A GOOD MAN IS HARD TO FIND"

MUGGSY SERENADES BUD AND JOE MARSALA

JOE MARSALA, BUD, AND PEE WEE

Sometimes Commodore used the CBS studios. Some old masters are still sitting up there waiting to be issued.

MORE OF "A GOOD MAN IS HARD TO FIND"

THE COMMODORE MUSIC SHOP WITH JOHNNY
WINDHURST, MILT GABLER, RED ALLEN, AND
EDDIE

Two views of a Decca recording session in 1950, with Cutty, Wild Bill, Peanuts, Gene Schroeder, Jack Lesberg, and Buzzy. This was my last date for Decca and we made tunes like "Maple Leaf Rag" and "Dill Pickles." Ralph Sutton was also on the date but he only played some solo things.

A Metronome All Star date. I didn't make this record but some of my pals did. Benny Carter, Jack Teagarden, Eddie Miller, and Benny Goodman seem happy about it. So does John Hammond.

GEORGE GERSHWIN
jazz
concert
directed by eddie condon
featuring lee wiley and a selected
group of jazz musicians
ALBUM NO. A-398 · 23M PERSONALITY SERIES
Decca
JACK TEAGARDEN • GUITAR • EDDIE CONDON • TRUMPET • BOBBY
AGARDEN • LOU McGARITY • BARITONE SAXOPHONE • ERNIE CACERES
• CLARINET • "PEE WEE" RUSSELL • EDMOND HALL • JOE DIXON
HONE • ERNIE CACERES • PIANO • JESS STACY
• JACK LESBERG • DRUMS • GEORGE WETTLING • JOHNNY

PLATTER PATTER

The album of Chicago Jazz, promised in December by Decca, finally has been released and is worth the long wait. Three studio bands cut 12 fine sides as follows: "Nobody's Sweetheart," "Friar's Point Shuffle," "There'll Be Some Changes Made" and "Someday Sweetheart" by Eddie Condon and his Chicagoans; "China Boy," "Jazz Me Blues," "Sugar" and "The World Is Waiting for the Sunrise" by Jimmy McPartland and his Orchestra; "Bugle Call Rag," "Sister Kate," "Darktown Strutters Ball" and "I've Found a New Baby" by George Wettling and his Chicago Rhythm Kings. The McPartland sides, cut in Chicago, have an advantage of good recording, something important to Chicago style, wherein final choruses find every man speaking his piece, although in closely integrated manner. The Condon band suffers most from lack of co-operation from the studio. However, all in all, the Condon sides must be called the best . . .

The piano of Joe Sullivan is perhaps the standout on the Condon waxings. Joe does his best work since recovering from his long illness, his crisply executed notes and clean phrasing edging Pee Wee Russell for honors. Pee Wee's gutteral clarinet shows to best advantage on "Friar's Point." Red McKenzie once remarked that Russell doesn't play from his heart, "he reaches right down to his socks," and when you hear Pee Wee here you know what Red means. The fine lead cornet of Maxie Kaminsky sets a bristling pace throughout each record, although the little man does fluff one note quite distinctly in "Friar's Point." The strictly Chicago tenor of Bud Freeman and the driving drums of Dave Tough, the guitar of Condon, the bass of Clyde Newcomb and the valve trombone of Brad Gowans complete the setup . . .

Biggest individual kick in the album is afforded by Jimmy McPartland. Jimmy almost makes Bix live again with a truly wonderful solo on "China Boy" and with his fine lead playing. His delicacy of phrasing and his Beiderbeckian tone lift the band well up there. His first chorus of "Sugar" remind one strongly of Bobby Hackett, his second more strongly of Bix. Bud Jacobson's clarinet a la Teschmaker, Boyce Brown's nice alto saxophone, Floyd Bean's tasteful piano, veteran Jim Lannigan's bass, Dick McPartland's guitar, and Hank Isaacs' drums contribute much.

Again piano and lead cornet take honors on the Wettling pressings, with Jess Stacy and Charlie Teagarden showing the way and with Wettling providing more subdued and more effective drumming than usual. Jess, of course, is tops, and "Little T" gets a chance to be himself, something Mr. P. W. seldom gives him. Joe Marsala, an excellent clarinetist in his own right, does some Freeman tenor tooting with a cleaner tone, and Danny Polo, remembered from the old Goldkette records, plays his clarinet with rare feeling. Floyd O'Brien contributes the only slide trombone chores of the album and in excellent fashion, too. Jack Bland plays guitar as he once did with McKenzie's Mound City Blue Blowers, and Artie Shapiro plucks the bass . . .

The album itself contains some intimate camera shots of the artists to be heard, made in the studios, and is attractively made, but the contents make the book worthwhile in any dress. After many playings the cornet of McPartland leaves the strongest impression, particularly to one who knows the playing of Bix. The Condon band has the best soloists—particularly Pee Wee, Bud and Joe. But there is much to be said for each side and for the album, another must for jazzophiles. It is recommended as an example—or eight of them—of just how lead cornet should be played. There isn't a high note in the book but the horn playing is forthright and unaffected, which is just as it should be.

The next time Milt let us into the studio we had almost the same band except Jack Teagarden had replaced Georg Brunis. The date was covered by *Life* magazine and Pee Wee was almost covered by some shylocks. He had been running up some pretty bad bills all over town and a gang of desperados were waiting to do him in. It took us longer than usual to get through his serenade.

Another *Life* party and Alex King even contributed the music. Alex did lots of things. I didn't know he wrote music. His royalty for the tune must have been at least thirty dollars.

The first "regulation size" Commodore record. They even put my name on it.

Another first. This was a four-part jam session we did in 1940 with double brass and triple reeds. Nobody else had the courage to try something like this until after the war.

We made four sides on this date. Fats Waller was under contract to Victor at the time so he named himself "Maurice" for the day.

Two sides for John Steinbeck

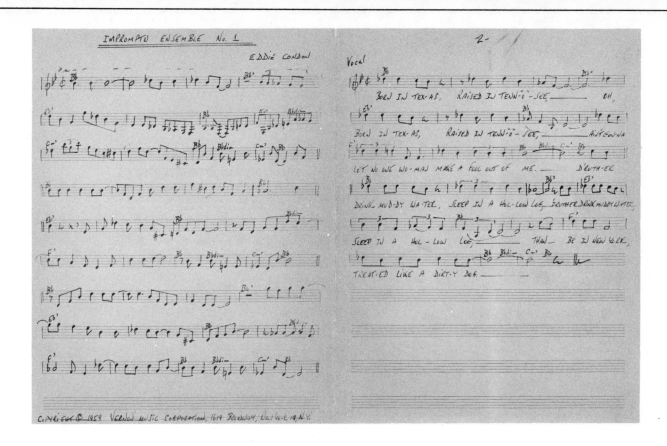

After he stopped working full time at his own label Milt Gabler joined Decca. The first thing he did was hire our guys, and we wound up with a series of good records. The title, "Impromptu Ensemble," was taken from the Town Hall jam sessions. Listener beware; this music was not written down until *after* we played it.

My favorite Lee Wiley vocal

Every time I write a book somebody names a record album after it. This was the first one.

The honor for the first "long-play" improvisation in jazz recording goes, of course, to the four twelve-inch, 78-rpm sides of "*A Good Man is Hard to Find*" that Eddie made for Commodore in 1940. It was Eddie's first session after the one we did together for the Chicago Jazz album, and I kidded him one night at Julius's about getting the idea from *Someday Sweetheart*, which ran too long on the first take.

We did a nice series of Condon LP's at Columbia and we attempted to use real programming conceptions. My favorite was *Jammin at Condon's*, based on the real-life happenings at the Sign of the Porkchop down on Third Street, where Eddie's house band was often visited by friends with happy results that we hoped we could reproduce in the studio. On this record the connection to Commodore's two front lines on *A Good Man is Hard to Find* is obvious, but instead of one long tune we were able to pick four long ones and a medley.

The Columbia series actually began with Eddie doing the eastern end of a coast-to-coast jam-session album (the other side was a group of Californians called the Rampart Street Paraders) in which the tone for the rest of the series was set by Eddie's credit line in the personnel listings. He was down as "guitar and conversations." We often left Eddie's spontaneous comments in if we caught something while the tapes were rolling. This was unheard-of at the time; if there was ever the slightest unplanned noise in the studio there was panic as far back as the reserve secretarial pool.

Eddie's recording dates were casual affairs. People dropped in the studio and as often as not there was an all-star cast on both sides of the microphone. We usually finished an album in two sessions even though the men got paid extra for recording more than the standard fifteen minutes for a three-hour date. The guys knew what they were doing. They knew that the extra bottle of Chivas Regal was waiting for them as soon as everything was wrapped up. The standard on the dates was three fifths, paced with care, and Eddie and I planned this as carefully as we planned personnels and routines. Before that we used to repair next door for recuperative rest periods. The Columbia studio on East Thirtieth Street is a former church and the building next to it is a former bank. The bank had converted to the saloon business but the stone over the entrance still says "BANK" and Eddie would often scoot next door with the guys to make a small withdrawal.

As much fun as the studio dates at Columbia were and later for World Pacific and Warner Brothers, the best recording was the first recording made at the Newport Jazz Festival in July 1955. The festival was in its second year and was shaky indeed. George Wein and Louis Lorillard welcomed my idea of recording Columbia artists at the festival in exchange for a donation.

Eddie was scheduled to open the first night. I sent engineers ahead with equipment while I accepted Eddie's invitation to ride up in a bus donated by the festival for his band. We hadn't counted on the festival drawing the way it did and by the time we poked along that narrow stretch of Route 138 to the ferry the clock was running and we were standing still. At the brink of the ferry we were stopped by an over-officious ferry-loader who bumped our bus in favor of several civilian cars. I called Louis Lorillard and he began threatening to have the ferry permanently discontinued if the bus was not on the next boat. He even arranged a police escort for us at the other end. By the time we landed it was starting to rain and the cops sloshed us through the thickening mud and we huddled in the musicians' tent. The engineers were worried because the equipment was getting wet and the wind was making its own harmonies across the open mikes. We eventually had to wrap nylon stockings around the mikes to serve as wind screens.

"Anybody without water wings keep your raincoats on," said Eddie, and cheers broke out when Gene Schroeder went out to check the piano. He reported it would be best to keep the top down so we had to mike it underneath the sounding board. "Well, things aren't all that bad," said Eddie. "They can't throw very well from under those ponchos." Eddie went out with the porkchop, put it on the piano top, and never unzipped the case. Serving only as traffic and water-safety director, he ran the guys through a set Johnny Weissmuller would have been proud of. No more to say; you can hear it all (with commentary) on the album.

—George Avakian

HOW TO MAKE A RECORD, AS SEEN BY RALPH BROOKS

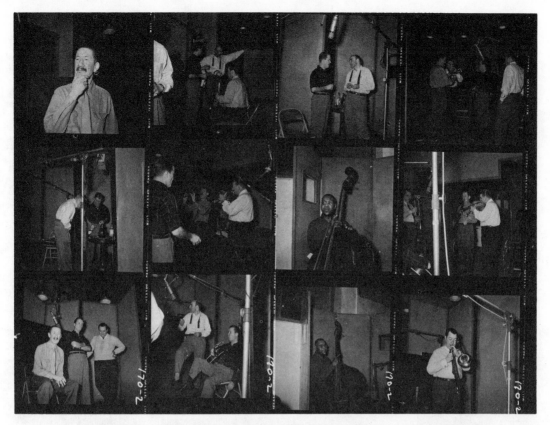

RECORDING WITH REX STEWART, DICK CARY AND CUTTY CUTSHALL

SAME DATE WITH ED HALL, LEONARD GASKINS AND BUD FREEMAN

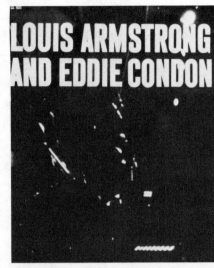

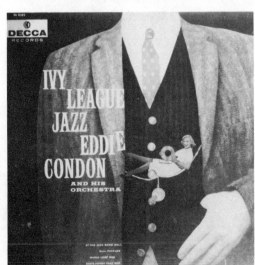

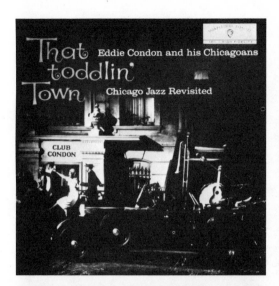

That toddlin' Town

EDDIE CONDON AND HIS CHICAGOANS

Chicago Jazz Revisited

CLUB CONDON

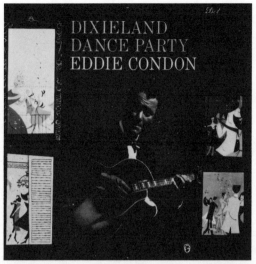

DIXIELAND DANCE PARTY

EDDIE CONDON

THE ROARING TWENTIES

EDDIE CONDON and his ALL-STARS

COLUMBIA

Oooo Oooo!! EDDIE CONDON ALL STARS TIGER RAG! & all that Jazz*

REX STEWART
BUD FREEMAN
CUTTY CUTSHALL
GEORGE WETTLING
HERB HALL
GENE SCHROEDER
LEONARD GASKIN

*
TIGER RAG
SENSATION RAG
LIVERY STABLE BLUES
LAZY DADDY
OSTRICH WALK
REISENWEBER RAG
BLUIN' THE BLUES
LAZY RIVER

FEATURING PEE WEE RUSSELL

BROTHER MATTHEW with Eddie Condon's Jazz Band

IELAND

in which

EDDIE CONDON

and his All-Stars

jam on a few of

"Bix Beiderbecke's favorites"

EDDIE CONDON

Condon a la carte

COMMODORE LP
FL 30.010

Eddie Condon and his

Strolling Reunion Commodores

with

Wild Bill Davison
Jeorg

How To Spell

Writing is not what I do best, but I can spell a little and with a patient editor I can usually put a few words together. The painful process has taken me through this, my third book, too many reviews and record columns to remember, commentary about my friends, and even writing liners for the back of record albums. Album liners are probably the worst chore in the world, second only to guessing who is playing on records or discussing jazz with semi-literate critics.

TORTILLA B FLAT

A serenade to John Steinbeck composed on the typewriter

BY EDDIE CONDON

I leave the saloon four-thirty, five o'clock in the morning and go home and read myself to sleep. Somehow I seem to read a lot of Johns: McNulty, Crosby, Dos Passos, Gunther, Chapman (I guess you count theatre critics writers) and O'Hara. John O'Hara still thinks I want to punch him in the nose because of a review he wrote in the New York *Times* about my book *We Called It Music*. It's not true. My nose-punching days are over. The only thing I thought about that review was they should have had O'Hara's picture at the top instead of mine because the review was more about O'Hara than it was about my book.

Steinbeck is my favorite John of all ever since John Hammond lent a copy of *In Dubious Battle* to a friend of mine named Harry Kruse and Harry lent it to me and I've still got it. I got a big jolt out of that book and from then on I was a Steinbeck man, which is funny when you think how I first met him.

It was in '42 or '43 and I was playing in Nick Rongetti's place in the Village and Bill Feinberg and his secretary Wanda Marvin came in with this big guy. Bill was a wheel in Local 802, the musicians' union, and he said he wanted me to meet the big guy. I took one look at him sitting there and although I heard the name I didn't hook it up. Bill didn't say this was Steinbeck the writer. I guess he figured I knew. I thought he was some kind of labor leader. (He used to be a day laborer, he told me later. He carried bricks, or laid them, for the building that is now Madison Square Garden.) So we sat around for a while talking and after while somebody said let's go over to Cafe Society.

At Cafe Society the first thing I knew I'd missed a set at Nick's. The reason I stayed so long was this big guy from California seemed to like the real American jazz. So we got to talking. Then I looked at my watch and figured I'd better get back to Nick's before Nick decided to get a new guitar player, so I went out. At the door I bumped into John Hammond, of all people, and I said there was a fellow over there sitting with Bill Feinberg, he's from the coast, seems like a nice fellow, name's Steinbeck. Hammond hollered *Steinbeck* and tore over to the table. I figured it was some old friend. Hammond's got more friends than I've busted guitar strings. I still didn't figure this big guy.

1 year or so later I was still playing in Nick's and in comes a fellow I used to room with in Chicago, Larry Kaiser. Says he's got Steinbeck from California with him, and to come over for a drink. My wife Phyllis was there that night and when the set ended I went over and sat with her at one of those little tables outside of Gents. Next thing this big guy comes over and puts his hand on my shoulder and says hello there. I said you're Steinbeck from California aren't you?

I still think he's some kind of union organizer. In fact, I think I remember Feinberg saying he's connected with some movie union. I said to him didn't he have something to do with the movies?

Well, indirectly, he said.

Naturally by then I'd read *The Grapes of Wrath* and I'd seen Hank Fonda in it in the movies, but I was still fogged up. Then I felt Phyllis kicking me under the table and all of a sudden I was out of the dark. I almost fell out of my chair. I said, Say you're not *The Grapes* Steinbeck, are you? He thought I said The Great. He said no, he was just John

Steinbeck. So we all went over to his table and from then on we got to know each other pretty well. That's the kind of fellow he is. You hear him talk, you'd never think he was anybody. You look at him, you'd never think he was a writer. Pee Wee Russell looks more like a writer.

Steinbeck hates to go to literary cocktail parties, but I got him to go to one, sort of, the day after I met him. I called him up and he said, hey, come on up and have a drink, so I went up to his hotel, the Bedford. Turned out we'd both forgotten it was some kind of election day. There wasn't a drop around anywhere, and you couldn't buy it. I got on the phone and made a few calls, but no use. Around that time John's literary agent, Annie Laurie Williams, she was also living at the Bedford, came in and said there's this cocktail party for some writer from England in the hotel, let's all go down there. You'd of taken oxen, you couldn't get John to go to anything like that. Then Annie Laurie said. Here's what I'll do, I'll go and get us a drink and bring them back here. She went and hooked a couple of jugs and brought them back, so we all sat around for a spell and talked about the real American jazz. That was how John went to his first literary party.

Couple of hours later some bow ties arrived. I always wear bows, always have since I was with the Hollis Peavey's Jazz Bandits. Last time I counted them I had sixty-five, not counting the ones at the cleaners and the ones I have at the saloon; my sister-in-law makes them for me. I saw those bow ties of Steinbeck's come in, I remembered he'd been wearing a four-in-hand the night before and I thought to myself, My God, am I influencing the guy already?

Main thing we talked about that day, Steinbeck said I ought to be playing banjo. He said the banjo is the only truly American instrument and he went into the history of the banjo considerably. I said, I stopped playing the banjo when everybody else did, shortly after I left Husk O'Hare, which was after I left Hollis Peavey, which was around 1924. The last banjo I had some landlord wound up with. Couple of months later he said to me again, Eddie, why don't you go back to the banjo? I said, John, the banjo went out with button shoes. He said, Eddie, button shoes are coming back.

Another topic outside of jazz that John and I always have in common, we both think that Joe Frisco is just about the funniest guy around. We always trade Joe Frisco stories. John told me one time he was sitting with Joe in some terrible joint in southern California, they were there for anthropological studies, and they noticed that the hostesses were only fourteen, fifteen years old, just kids. Steinbeck started feeling paternal and sorry for them and said, Joe, look at those children, look at that one girl over there, look how young she is. That child ought to be in bed. Joe Frisco said, I th-think th-that c-could b-be a-arranged.

Couple of times I've tried to talk to John about his writing. Might as well try to play harp with the Philharmonic; he won't talk about it at all, he's too modest. Any time I ever say to him, John, I like such and such a book, he changes the subject to jazz. He's really a nut on jazz; told me once he had some records I made that I'd forgot the titles of. Well, the other day I made a list of John's stuff that I like best, and since I can't tell him I'll put it in here:

1. *In Dubious Battle*. (Guess you always like the first book you read of any writer's the best.) 2. That thing he wrote about the Sea of Cortez with the guy who was nuts about fish. Some parts of that were beyond me; as far as fish are concerned, I even get confused in front of a goldfish bowl. 3. *Cannery Row* and *Tortilla Flat*. (I put these two together because after I read them I swore off wine forever. Wine reminds me of a friend of mine, a singer, he drank it all the time.) 4. *The Moon Is Down*. (John autographed this one to me. He spelled New York "Ney York.") 5. *Burning Bright*. (Haven't finished this newest one yet because I started reading it on the way back from a job down South my boys and I played. I figure I either left it on the plane or that Peanuts Hucko, the honest clarinet player, stole it because he likes John too. What I think about this book, you take a girl and you put her together with three guys, two of them are bound to finish last.)

One time some of the boys and I were up at Commodore Records, cutting some sides, and we figured we better do something for this Steinbeck so we made up a blues—he likes blues best—called Tortilla B Flat. Next time Steinbeck and I ran into each other, he just grinned. One thing about him, he can say as much by an expression as most people can with a couple hundred words.

What very few people know is that I got into television after the war on account of John. I'd been on Gilbert Seldes' CBS programs just before the war, but then after Pearl Harbor came along and the TV time was cut, nothing. After the war a guy named Henry White called me up one day and said Steinbeck suggested that he and I get together and talk about television. He said Steinbeck was interested in an outfit called World Video, one of the silent sponsors or something. So that afternoon this Henry White and I met up at John's house and the next thing I knew I was in TV with my boys. Another thing John was partly responsible for my getting into was the writing business. One time I was at a party at Tim Costello's saloon for John McNulty's book, *Third Avenue, New York,* and some guy from a publishing house came up to me and said, When are you going to write a book about yourself? I looked at him, said, The whiskey here's strong but it can't be that strong. After that some other guy approached me and finally I asked Steinbeck how you go about writing a book. He said, Why, you just sit down and write it.

Tom Sugrue and I sat down, but it wasn't as easy as John made it sound. Later I found out Steinbeck doesn't do it that way either. Sometimes he worries a whole day over just one sentence, or a word in a sentence. Maybe that's why the stuff he writes makes me feel as though I was there. You can't ask any more of a writer.

Since John was partially responsible for me moving into his field, I've been figuring out a way to trap him into mine. I'm going to send him a banjo if I can find one. Maybe some night he'll come into my place, the banjo under his arm, and sit down and play with the boys. Wearing button shoes, naturally.

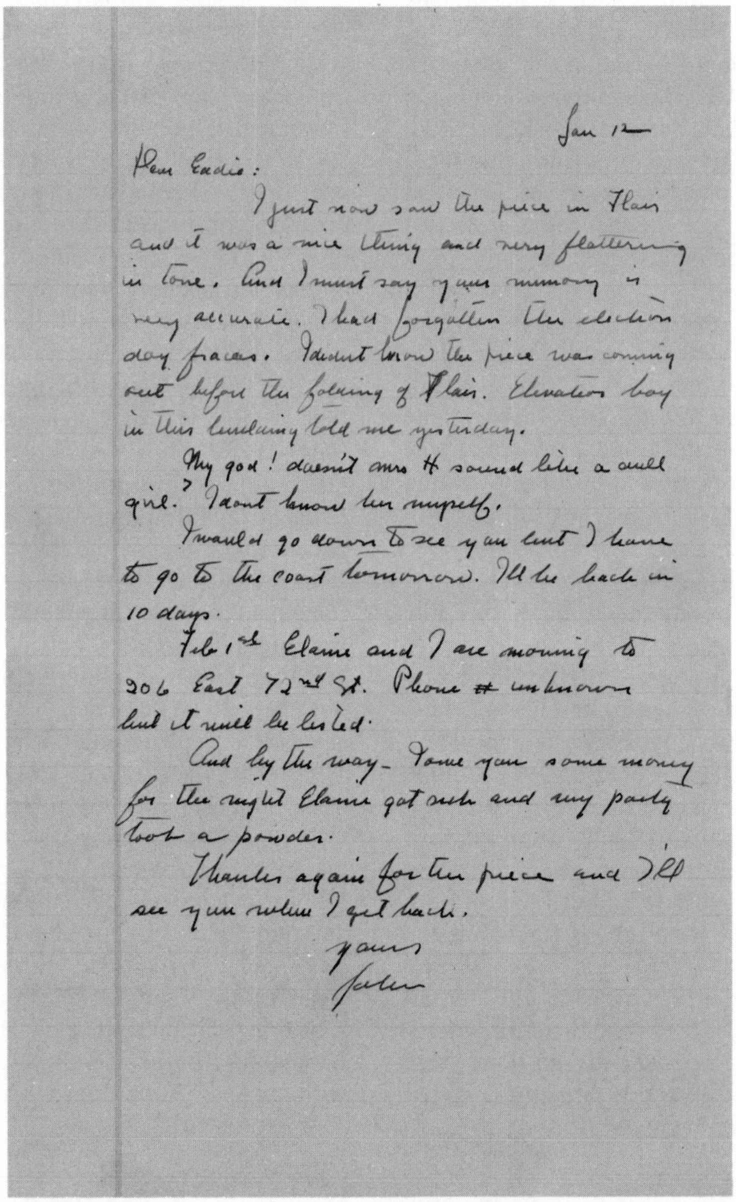

Jan 12

Dear Eadie:

I just now saw the piece in *Flair* and it was a nice thing and very flattering in tone. And I must say your memory is very accurate. I had forgotten the election day fracas. I didnt know the piece was coming out before the folding of *Flair*. Elevator boy in this building told me yesterday.

My god! doesn't mrs H sound like a dull girl? I dont know her myself.

I would go down to see you but I have to go to the coast tomorrow. I'll be back in 10 days.

Feb 1st Elaine and I are moving to 206 East 72nd St. Phone # unknown but it will be listed.

And by the way—I owe you some money for the night Elaine got sick and my party took a powder.

Thanks again for the piece and I'll see you when I get back.

yours
John

In 1947 Tom Sugrue and I put a book together. It was honest and sold a few copies.

Eddie Condon: "Guitar Player, Impresario, Defender, Apologist and Publicist in the Field of Pure Jazz."

67

A High Priest of Jazz Sets Down His Life Story

WE CALLED IT MUSIC. By Eddie Condon. Narration by Thomas Sugrue. 341 pp. New York: Henry Holt & Co. $3.

By JOHN O'HARA

SOME thirty years ago, in a little coal-mining town in the anthracite region of Pennsylvania, there lived a boy, a boy of 12. He was tall for his age, and in many ways precocious. He looked forward to the day when he, like Clint Sheafer, would own his own Mercer; when, like Al Cullum, he would be on his way to Yale; when, like Bill Ulmer, he would know the 16th Arrondissement better than he knew the Third Ward. He had, this boy, no scorn for the tokens of high living. To be greeted by name at the Bellevue-Stratford; to be able to charge trinkets at Bailey, Banks & Biddle; to command the services of Wimley, the caterer, and Battle, the florist; to summon forty or fifty of the horsey to steak and potatoes at Elkins Park—these things were in the dreams of this boy.

But his dreams were not all of dukes and 'lords and Russian czars and men who owned their motor cars. One day he would grow to manhood, and he would lead, of all things, not his people in rebellion against the hated Sassenach; not his class in the polling for Biggest Snake; not Schuylkill County in the race for Prothonotary. No, one day he would lead a jazz band!

The years have passed, thirty in number, and this reviewer never has owned a Mercer, gone to Yale, identified the 16th from any other arrondissement, been greeted by name at the Bellevue, charged anything at Bailey's,

hired Wimley or Battle, eaten a meal in Elkins Park, nor led a jazz band, except, in the latter case, against the protests of the bandsmen. The sad, sad thing, moreover, is that not one of those things matters any more. It is awfully hard, therefore, for this reviewer to get excited one way or the other about "We Called It Music," a kind of autobiography of Eddie Condon with what is called a "narration" by Thomas Sugrue.

ONE day, presumably, Mr. Condon got up and walked around the room, decided that he had had an interesting life, and sat right down again and commenced to write it. Somewhere along the line, presumably, he decided that he needed a competent collaborator, and he certainly acquired one in Mr. Sugrue. The resulting autobiography is in roman and the narration is in italics; there is a discography, which means a list of phonograph records; the book has some photographs, an index, and a family tree.

Eddie Condon js a good, steady guitar player who was born Albert Edwin Condon on Nov. 16, 1905, in Benton County, Indiana. All his life he has been knocking around among jazz musicians. His special fame is not owing to his standing as a guitar player but rather to his efforts as impresario, defender, apologist, and publicist in the field of pure jazz —so long as the purity is attested by Condon himself. Mr. Sugrue, at one point in his narration, declares of Condon and the music he likes: "He even gave' his

identity to it. People referred to him as 'Mr. Jazz.'" Well, I can't say that I ever heard Mr. Condon referred to as "Mr. Jazz," but it is equally true that I never heard anyone else referred to as "Mr. Jazz." (One painfully shy radio couple do call themselves Mr. and Mrs. Music.)

In the past ten years, give or take a couple, Eddie Condon has taken on a sort of playing-captain job in jazz. As a rule he surrounds himself with a group of fine jazz musicians, such as Bill Davison, Bobby Hackett, Max Kaminsky, Joe Bushkin, Gene Schroeder, Art Hodes, James P. Johnson, Pee Wee Russell, Sidney Bechet, Bud Freeman, George Wettling, Joe Sullivan (to be sure), Bob Casey, Dave Tough, Miff Mole, Brad Gowans and others who drop in to sit in. There is now a saloon called Eddie Condon's in Greenwich Village where eligible (invited) musicians may perform, and the more or less regulars sometimes are joined for fun by visiting artists like Tommy Dorsey. Like Tommy Dorsey, if any. The tunes they play are pretty much the same tunes year in, year out, and the truth is they play them pretty much the same way (although that will be denied), but what they play they play marvelously well.

The recurring, disloyal suspicion that John Corigliano could pick eight or ten men out of the Philharmonic and get the same results has no place here except as an example of the kind of thinking Condon has been fighting all these years. Surely Tossy Spivakovsky can do anything Joe

Venuti can do, and not only because Spivakovsky's curious fingering and bowing make his performance look harder. For that matter there is, or used to be (I haven't been in the place in five years), a drummer with the Radio City Music Hall band who is at least the equal of Gene Krupa or Chauncey Moorehouse, but you might have a hard time convincing Condon.

THIS devotion to jazz is all right. It is understandable, and, at long last, it is paying off. I don't know, though, about the autobiography part. What the autobiographer remembers as the fascinating life of a fascinating man seems to me to have been rather ordinary, in spite of the fact that Condon apparently remembers every wjsecrack he ever made (in recalling exchanges of wit he never gives himself any the worst of it), every Society character he ever met (and he includes some lulus as Society people); and an all-around prankishness which, I infer, Condon offers as evidence of the artistic temperament.

There must be hundreds, nay, millions who have been wanting to know more about Eddie Condon, and for them this is the book. But the book is not specifically recommended to admirers of Dick McDonough, Django Reinhardt, Albert Casey, Carl Kress, Perry Botkin, Blackface Eddie Ross, Freddie Green, Clarence Haliday, Lawrence Lucie, Carmen Mastren, or even Mike Pingatore, George Van Eps, or Eddie Peabody. They all played guitar, and they are not mentioned.

6

John O'Hara's review of my book in the
New York Sunday Times Book Review

Goodman's 'Benny' Fitted

—By EDDIE CONDON—

BENNY GOODMAN opened recently in his first New York engagement in a long, long time. I asked Pete Pesci to mind the store and went uptown on safari to see him.

"I'll mind the store," Pete said, but who's going to mind you?"

Benny was playing at Basin Street, which is Ralph Watkins' new version of a room that's had more names than Jane Russell has admirers. The room was loaded, and a large crowd was trying to follow suit.

Whenever I see Benny I remember the Winter in Chicago when we were new to the world and jazz music was too. I had a girl named Barbara whom I'd met at a lake the Summer before. She came from a family who were never faced with a shortage of ready trump. When I knew her, Barbara was between finishing schools. The family wasn't exactly wild to have their little girl playing nosey-nosey with a banjo player.

BENNY GOODMAN

Put it this way: her mother couldn't stand me, and I was equally impressed.

Needed Overcoat

Barbara and I took to having clandestine meetings on street corners. Everything was going along all right until cold weather came. I had a jacket that was fairly presentable, and a pair of halfway decent tights, but I had no overcoat.

Benny, in those days, had some overcoat connections—a sister in the business, or something. Of course he'd always been a good wage earner from the teething ring up, and so he always had a coat. It was just my size.

Benny and I used to meet over at the musicians' union headquarters, he'd give me the coat, and I'd sail off to meet Barbara. It was a tubular coat, a perfect fit. I always had a feeling that if Barbara's mother could have seen me in it, she might have got over her prejudice against banjo players.

Well, Benny's grown a lot since those days, in biceps as well as finance. I certainly wouldn't want to meet any girls in his coat now.

The other night at Basin Street I was glad to see that Benny was still playing as exciting as he did in the coat-trading days. Mel Powell is with him, playing some superior

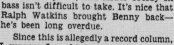

JUDY GARLAND

Mel Powell piano, and Israel Crosby on bass isn't difficult to take. It's nice that Ralph Watkins brought Benny back—he's been long overdue.

Since this is allegedly a record column, I suppose I ought to mention some of Benny's sides here. When they give me the whole paper to do it in, I will. He's made them for Columbia, RCA-Victor, Capitol—name the label, and Benny's occupied it. Right now, the Columbia albums of his Carnegie Hall concerts in the late thirties are outselling even his recent stuff.

* * *

THE WEEK'S CROP isn't anything to rave about. HEY THERE and THIS IS MY BELOVED, by Sammy Davis, Jr., with orchestra directed by Sy Oliver, is one they say will be a hit. This is a departure, this record, for both names. Sy Oliver, a fine arranger for Jimmie Lunceford and later Tommy Dorsey, here turns his hand to strings. Sammy Davis, Jr., is generally heard and seen with several blood relatives—his father and Will Masten, his uncle. I've seen them on television, as who hasn't? Davis comes through better when you see him. On records, he sounds like Nat "King" Cole has joined the Marines. It's a Decca release.

JOEY and AND SO I WALKED HOME, by Betty Madigan, with orchestra conducted by Joe Lipman (MGM). First side is going great in the coin boxes. I suppose I ought to admire it, since I'm Irish only on my father's and mother's sides, but I can't work up any great sweat of enthusiasm.

BETTY MADIGAN

THE MAN THAT GOT AWAY and HERE'S WHAT I'M HERE FOR, by Judy Garland, with orchestra conducted by Ray Heindorf (Columbia). Both songs are from Mrs. Sid Luft's new picture, "A Star Is Born." She is just good enough to pull through this material. Once again there are about a thousand people wailing in the background, making the record a boxing match with too many contestants. It's a tribute to Judy's lung power that she can make herself heard.

If the record companies are wondering what to give me for Labor Day, I have my present all picked out. I'd like a nice record sung straight with a straight accompaniment—with no wind chamber, no chorus, no battery of fiddles—nothing but music.

NEXT WEEK: "I'm Gonna Scrub That Man Right Outa My Scalp," by Joe Holman, Jr., and his Nashville Bloody Mary Bombers, with vocals by Les Forrester.

Critic and His Helpers

—By EDDIE CONDON—

WHATEVER may be said about this week's patch, nobody can say I didn't have adequate assistance. While Daddy set up the phonograph in the yard, Maggie and Liza, aged nine and eleven, and Phyllis, by profession their mother, and Punchy, the beagle, all came to help.

There was also some aid from John Windhurst, a trumpet player, Estelle Parsons of NBC, the Monmouth Beach wind, and a Mr. Begg of Glasgow, Scotland.

Some friend had sent Liza a record. "Daddy, can we play my record?" she asked.

Daddy said,

VAUGHN MONROE

"Later," and got onto the first business at hand, THEY WERE DOING THE MAMBO, recorded by Vaughn Monroe with Orchestra (RCA-Victor).

They tell me this is one of the biggest things in the juke boxes right now. All I know about Monroe is that for years he sold cigarettes—but the only people who got cancer from him were people with ears.

The other side is MISTER SANDMAN, also by Old Hairy Tonsils. A better name for this would be MR. SANDTHROAT. It isn't a bad tune, though. I hear this is a comeback for Monroe, and I can't help wondering if this trip was really necessary.

"Daddy, can we play my record?" Liza asked.

"After we play HERNANDO'S HIDEAWAY," Daddy said, and did. This is by Archie Bleyer, an orchestra and chorus, with a castanet solo by Maria Alba (Cadence label).

Maggie recognized the tune. Maggie goes to the Star of the Sea Academy in Monmouth Beach, and there are some little Spanish girls in her class.

"They go wild over this one," Maggie said.

"Daddy what about my record?" Liza said.

ARCHIE BLEYER

"Punchy, stop barking," Phyllis said.

"Anybody in for Mr. Begg?" Windhurst said.

"A record like that might go great in Spain," Estelle said.

Daddy agreed with all statements, including the last. The reverse of HERNANDO'S HIDEAWAY is also Archie Bleyer, this time featuring a trumpet solo by James Burke. The title is S'IL VOUS PLAIT. To show how qualified I am to review this French tune, I thought it was Italian.

"Daddy, what about my ——?"

Before Liza could finish, I put on Hugo Winterhalter's THE LITTLE SHOEMAKER (RCA-Victor). I took it right off again, too. The most distressing thing about this is that it's current. I can't face the thought of going through a revival of it in a couple of years. The other side, also with Mr. Winterhalter and Chorus, is THE MAGIC TANGO.

The label also says the group is assisted by "a Friend." That's nice; but I doubt if he'll have any left after this pair.

Maggie and Liza overturned two of the lawn chairs. "We're making a chair house," Maggie said.

"Go and play in the real house," Daddy said.

"Daddy, are you ever going to play my record?" Liza asked.

"Punchy, stop barking," Daddy said. "Phyllis, is there anything we can do about Punchy?"

"Why don't you review HIM?" Phyllis suggested helpfully.

"You can't review a dog," I said.

How wrong I was! The next selection was ANGELA MIA and CRAZY 'BOUT YA BABY, by a group called The Crew Cuts. This record is a real dog if I've ever heard one—and I've heard Punchy.

I hope The Crew Cuts have a lot of wealthy relatives, because I don't think they can expect to make a living doing that. There must be a lot of optimistic people over at the Mercury Company. After these guys, Vaughn Monroe sounds almost as good to me as the late Red McKenzie.

PUNCHY
The Critic

"Daddy, please may we play my record now?" Liza asked.

Punchy barked his agreement. That was enough for Daddy. Gathering together records, paper, typewriter and Mr. Begg, he moved into the real house.

By that time I felt a little punchy myself.

Singers in Wind Tunnel

—By EDDIE CONDON—

IT often seems to me that straight singers and musicians have just about vanished off the face of the earth.

These days you can't be a singer unless you operate in a wind tunnel, or death chamber, or whatever it is they call those caves over at the recording studios.

EDDIE CONDON

And you can't be a musician unless you've got four or five electric cords trailing off your instrument and two more plugged into your ears.

After listening to some of the current records I can't help thinking how nice it would be if somebody just sat down and sang a straight song with a nice, easy instrumental accompaniment. Even a ukulele would be preferable to one of those electrical devices.

Some of the old Negro bands used to use a washboard for rhythm.

Today, from the way they sound, they use washing machines.

All of which brings us to a small crop of atrocities that came for review this week. Pardon me while I plug in my nose:

NAPOLEON and MONDAY SERENADE, by Mitch Miller and Orchestra (Columbia). There are a tremendous number of people yelling and playing things that sound like Hawaiian-style harpsichords in this one.

I hope it isn't intended for juveniles, because the authorities have been having enough trouble with that problem.

Mitch Miller, popular recording director for Columbia, has committed as much mayhem on modern popular music as anybody around. This won't cause his reputation to suffer.

EARTHA KITT

EASY DOES IT and MINK SCHMINK, by Eartha Kitt, with Henri Rene (RCA-Victor). My friend Dick Gehman once said "Eartha Kitt" sounded like something a geologist would take along on a rock-hunt.

Considering this lady's charm, anybody would be glad to have her along on any kind of hunt . . . as long as she kept quiet.

Miss Kitt has a tremulo that many people find appealing. They must; she's very, very popular. To me, that tremulo sounds as though she was recording during a stickup.

IN THE SHADE OF THE OLD APPLE TREE and MANANA, by Pete Rugolo and His Orchestra (Columbia). Rugolo used to arrange for Stan Kenton, and turned out some very nice things. This has a good beat and very little of that offensive electricity.

There must be 17 or 18 guys in this band. It's quite difficult to make that many men sound agreeable, even with one another. Rugolo does it. The first side is straight, and the second is a little bopperiner. Not too hard to take. .

ANGELS IN THE SKY and BOULEVARD OF NIGHTINGALES, by Tony Martin and Henri Rene (he's recording everything this week) and His Orchestra. Well, you only have to hear a note or two of this one to know it isn't Burl Ives.

Peter Pesci, who is the manager of Condon's Downtown Club for Older Disabled Boys, used to go to sleep at night with Tony Martin records under his money belt.

He could have made a worse choice. Martin is one of the few men around who sings like a man and not like a Waring Mixer. He's at his best on these two.

BABY DON'T DO IT and I AIN'T GOT THE MAN, by Jaye P. Morgan with an orchestra conducted by Frank De Vol (Derby). This pair reminds me of Connie's Inn, around 1929. They used to have great floor shows there, and there was always a Negro girl singer who sounded like this.

This is good rough-shod music, with everybody having a fine time.

It's too bad they don't have Recordvision, for this girl must put on quite a show.

Wait a minute. I just took another look at the name of this lady.

Jaye P. Morgan.

With a voice like that one, big and broad as it is, I don't see much chance of her ever getting a midget on her lap.

* * *

NEXT WEEK: Several of the newer releases by the Mayor of Huntington Park, California, Hollis Peavey and his Jazz Bandits.

TONY MARTIN

Frank Conniff thought I ought to write a record-review column in the early fifties. He asked me to meet him one day and outline a format. I did and this is what happened. Dick Gehman and all the record companies helped out. Dick helped me spell and the record companies kept sending me bad records to review.

Phyllis and the Kids

Every scrapbook like this has a mandatory family section. Phyllis Condon is in charge of family matters at the Condon household so we simply told her she was also in charge of putting a few words together to headline the section. She jumped at the assignment and, like the true TV and magazine writer she is, started out by saying, "The gleaming highlights of those music-filled years float around in my subconscious like bright party lanterns in a foggy sky."

We told her to cut out the baloney so she dug up some great material she had written some years back for some lady's magazine. It says it all and has been retitled, "I Go Steady With Eddie."

Eddie was just sixteen when he started travelling with a hotsy-totsy Mississippi River jazz band back in Illinois. They billed him as The World's Youngest Banjo Player. Since then Eddie has absorbed thirty-some years of hard and joyful living, yet he still has the look of that beamish boy with the banjo—with his sporty bow ties, his dapper haberdashery, his electric way of skittering and darting around a room, and his baffling staccato talk. His friends from Chicago days still call him "Slick." And if you ask me, there's nobody in the world that glib syllable fits better than Eddie. After all these years I still can't tune in on his special slick, high-speed view of life.

Eddie was thirty-six when I first met him at a Hickory House Jam Session. I wasn't too dumb to see that he'd never taken up the habit of steady girls. My guess was that serious romance didn't fit in with Eddie's budget, his off-beat wildness, or his free-lance bachelor ways. There seemed to be absolutely no way to motivate a "date" with Eddie.

But I did make a discovery. Eddie didn't have an alarm clock in his cage (that's what he called his cheap two-by-four room in a West Side fleabag hotel.) The girls on the switchboard were too busy to be nursemaids to all those sleepy trombone players and dizzy drummers so Eddie often slept right through some dazzling afternoon social function over at the Colony, at some showgirl's flat, or in Tim Costello's damp dark-whiskyish saloon. He did, that is, until he met me. I guess I looked like the reliable sensible ground-gripper-type of broad. So Eddie asked me one night if I'd mind calling him on the phone promptly at three o'clock the next day, from my office in the advertising copy department at Wanamaker's Store. He had a sizzling date he didn't want to miss. *Would* I? I certainly *would*. And that's how I did it.

I became "the gentle voice from nowhere." The sentimental alarm clock poke in his fancy detached ribs. That single phone call soon became a daily one. Then a perfect lead-in to a daily five o'clock date. I was pretty sneaky and in no time at all, it took me everywhere.

Backstage at the Paramount to meet Frank Sinatra. To cocktails at Sardi's with Burgess Meredith, Henry Fonda, Bing Crosby, or Lord Donegal. And finally down to a back-street church near Washington Square (picked out of the yellow pages) to be married on Eddie's thirty-seventh birthday. It had seemed as inconceivable to get the slippery Eddie down to City Hall for a marriage license as to catch a hummingbird with a saltshaker. But I did it—and it was fun.

I remember the afternoon of my first date with Eddie. All dates with musicians, except on Sundays, have to be in the afternoon. He took me to his favorite eating spot, a narrow barren stand-up dairy bar on Sixth Avenue, at 49th street. He called it simply "The Milk Store." The place was shaped like a caboose and about as glamorous as a hardware loft, but it was the in-place for musicians to cluster at dusk to cool their throats with the pure white balm of cow's milk. I'd been daydreaming of a rendezvous with the famous, scintillating Eddie in some 52nd Street bistro with wine and fun and jazz. Instead, he handed me one of the two tabloids he'd picked up on the corner, asked me if I preferred cheese or liverwurst on rye, buttermilk or plain milk, propped his newspaper on the counter in front of him and then said, "What do you say we take the subway up to 135th street? Fats Waller is giving his boy a piano lesson and we can listen." I felt as if Valentino had just dragged me into his tent.

Fun is the most important thing in Eddie's life. When he laughs he fizzes all over with joy. When he tells a story he gets with it so deeply it's like an anaesthetic. When he plays his guitar he's completely drowned in some inner personal effervescence—some mysterious fizz.

At home our life is about as formal as Huckleberry Finn's. Neighbors call it queer, hippyish, crazy. We just think of it as free, convenient and all our own. We have no regular schedules or set hours for doing things. I work from nine or ten till five writing Coca Cola stuff in an advertising agency. Eddie operates on the late lobster shift, and our ten-and twelve-year-old daughters, Maggie and Liza, have still another day-span. They eat, relax, go to school and play like other normal children, by the clock. To them, Eddie is just Uncle DaDa, a wonderful Irish friend of ours who's always game to cancel a date, miss a boat, or throw the contract out the window just to have a ball.

After Maggie and Liza were born we found a long, cool, old-fashioned nine-room apartment on Washington Square, up to then the New York pad of Amy Vanderbilt. We still live there.

Through our front windows we look out on the leafy green treetops of Washington Square in summer and in winter, on cheerful scenes of children, park-sitters, and brightly-clad strollers in the snow. Nearby, the famous old Minetta elm that was a gallows tree in Colonial days and later provided welcome shade for General Washington and his troops almost brushes against our window panes—seems close enough to touch. Romantic scenes like those John Sloan painted in the early days of the century, when he lived in a house just down the block, still lure us into sentimental reveries whenever we sit on our window-sills. Mark Twain once lived next door, Henry James across MacDougal alley.

Bing Crosby is Liza's godfather and christening day down on Washington Square was like a Keystone Comedy—but serious. Bing was stopping at the Waldorf in New York and missing his workout on the golf course at Pebble Beach. So on the morning of the ceremony he decided to walk the fifty blocks down to Washington Square, just for exercise. He wore a leather windbreaker and khaki janitor's hat instead of his usual gaudy haberdashery. It was really a better disguise than a false moustache for Der Bingle. Not one autograph hunter or dear-old-college-chum stopped him on the way.

These were the plans we had made: We were to bring the baby down to the apartment lobby at ten A.M., where we would meet Bing and walk together over to St. Joseph's. He arrived at 9:45 and sat down in the lobby to rest. Beside him sat a photographer from *The Daily News,* tipped off by Eddie's press agent. There the two of them lounged, waiting for the entourage to begin. The photographer was lugging a big carton of bulbs and a box camera. They both looked strange, but happy and anxious to please. The building superintendent had other ideas. He came out, looked at the big box and said, "You might as well get going boys. The exterminators went through this building yesterday." Bing said, "OK Dad," and went out to wait on the sidewalk.

A while later we stumbled into a lucky break on a big old-fashioned country house out on the Jersey Shore. We'd been spending our summers in rundown, rented Charles Addams houses along the ocean front. We liked to splash around in the sun and salt water, but didn't like the fancy high-bracket rents. Then one hot afternoon a neighborhood real estate fella came strolling out to the beach to tell me that he thought the people across the way were putting their house on the market. It was a big white Dutch Colonial place with old Kentucky mint julep pillars, plenty of green hedges, and an acre or so of grassy lawn. To me, its wide, comfortable mansard roof had always seemed to have a kind, protective feeling. Not exactly beautiful—but big, ample and friendly. Immediately in my mind's eye, I saw our red and yellow croquet set staked out in the broad backyard. I imagined a family picnic out under the sycamore trees. I saw us, the Condons, and all our cousins, gathered round the cozy red brick fireplace I'd seen through the big windows at night.

One hour and ten minutes later I phoned Eddie in New York. "Eddie," I said, "you just bought a house. A big white thirteen-room house with pillars." "Good," said Eddie. "What else is new?"

Eddie has no ulcers, wrinkles or gray hair and all 32 teeth. I suppose this is because he ignores clocks, schedules, time tables, musical scores, and all other man-made plans. He ignores, in particular, the arrival and departure time of boats, planes, trains and buses. The trains he does catch make him very happy. Those he misses are okay too. Once in a while, after the Condon Club closes at three o'clock Sunday morning, and he's missed the last common carrier headed for home, he resorts to plan B. He phones for a limousine. When the car arrives around dawn at our door in Monmouth Beach, he's usually passed out among the back cushions, with nothing in his pockets but his night's accumulation of "memos" and the two-dollar bus fare he borrowed from the till. When this happens the forty-dollar fare, collected by the chauffeur on delivery, comes out of a special family sugar bowl, known to me privately as "Track and Cadillac Money" or the "Who Does He Think He Is Anyhow, A Millionaire?" fund.

On my 49th birthday, the best present I got was an all-out non-stop real-live Johnny Mercer song-fest. It was Sunday and at five in the morning Eddie arrived as usual at the Jersey Shore. He came up to my room and said, "Get up, Phyllis, there's a present for you downstairs." "Animal or mineral?" I asked. "Human," said Ed. I got up, put on a housecoat and started to comb my hair and put on lipstick. Eddie yelled, "Where do you think you're going—to the Met? Go down as you are!" "What? And frighten the human?" I said. "This is only a fella," said Ed. When I came down there was Johnny Mercer standing in the kitchen eating an orange. I knew right then it was going to be a birthday to remember. By three in the afternoon the band began to assemble. Pee Wee Russell, Johnny Windhurst, my brother Paul on guitar, brother Sid on suitcase and Wild Bill Davison were there and Johnny Mercer sang, hummed and improvised for hours. He sang his own songs. His own were the only ones he fluffed the words on! So he just made up new ones. For the house full of kids he sang crazy tunes, folk songs and old Savannah sketches. Everybody there took a turn doing a single. Even I sang, "Wal I Swan" and "Sweetheart if you Talk in Your Sleep—Don't Mention My Name," in my wavering off-key falsetto.

In the City—Eddie always prefers a nice cool subway to rattling around in New York taxis. He never carries a billfold and is rarely caught with any currency bigger than a five-dollar bill. He's known as a free pourer at his own place, though, and will sign a tab at the drop of an ice cube when he's socializing at 21.

Like me, Eddie spends about three days a week in the country, wallowing in Jersey peaches, ripe red tomatoes, Jersey butter-milk, children, beagles, and salt air. He's never been domestic or handy around the house. The lid to our carpenter kit bears the plan label, "Mrs. Condon's Tool Chest." And that's exactly what it is. Behind the wheel of a car he's enough to give anyone a nervous breakdown. Never knows which turn to take to the post office, the church or the general store.

Eddie thrives on the bucolic life, yet can't stand to spend more than a few days away from the magic island of Manhattan. Its music, its chaos, its perpetual change and motion, its never ending carnival is definitely his dish. Even though he calls me Bessie Burbank or The Wild Rose of Washington Square, I think he likes the garden. One afternoon I actually caught him down on his knees in the zinnias, pulling out wild carrot and ragweed roots. He looked up, coughed, said "Bring me a vodka"—then "Say, why didn't somebody tell me? This dirt smells swell!"

If we looked silly, it was justified. We had been married one hour before, on my thirty-seventh birthday.

Prenourishment: Phyllis, one month before Maggie

One day before Maggie

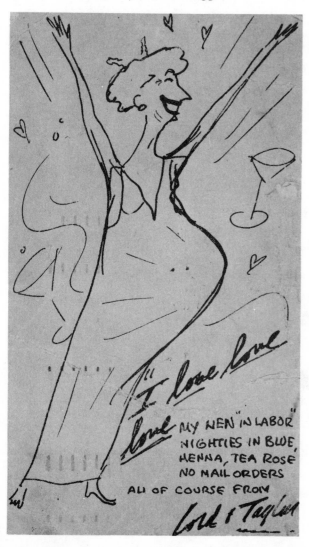

"I love love love MY NEN "IN LABOR" NIGHTIES IN BLUE, HENNA, TEA ROSE NO MAIL ORDERS ALL OF COURSE FROM *Lord & Taylor*

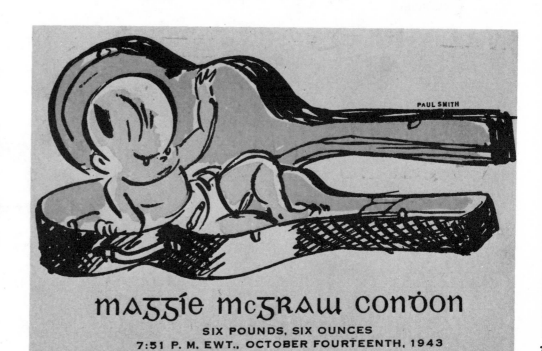

PAUL SMITH

maggie mcgraw condon

SIX POUNDS, SIX OUNCES
7:51 P. M. EWT., OCTOBER FOURTEENTH, 1943

PHYLLIS, BING, PHYLLIS (SMITH) MITCHELL, FR. MCCAFFREY,
LIZA, EDDIE

When Muggsy was in town he would come
by every Sunday and take Maggie and Liza
to his mother's house for coconut cake. The
kids still remember. The cake must have
been good.

The girls liked to play on the beach at our house in Monmouth Beach.

Phyllis liked to stay inside. Here with Misha Reznikoff.

Family portrait with Johnny Mercer and Paul Smith

On Washington Square

Monmouth Beach

Father and Mother with their two banditeers

Walt Kelly came by the club once. He likes jazz too.

Phyllis by Julian Levy

Winter off Washington Square

This picture is out of focus. So is Phyllis.

With Squirrel at Pike Lake

(Left) *The tie—a gift from Johnny Mercer*

Eddie Condon Prepares Favorite Dish

RUMSON — Jazzman - restaurateur Eddie Condon combines scalloped potatoes and Vienna sausages in Condon's Magic Casserole, one of his specialties which is a family favorite. He prepares it when the family gather weekends in their home at 125 Avenue of the Two Rivers.

Condon's Magic Casserole
3 cups sliced raw potatoes
8 Vienna sausages, diced
1 can sliced mushrooms (8 oz.)
sliced mushrooms (8 oz.), 1 tea-
1 teaspoon salt
⅛ teaspoon pepper
3 tablespoons minced onion
1 can evaporated milk
1 tomato sliced
¼ cup grated American cheese (1 oz.)

Arrange about half potato slices, sausages, and mushrooms in a greased casserole. Sprinkle with half the salt, pepper, and onion. Repeat. Pour milk over all. Cover and bake 45 minutes at 350 degrees.

Remove from oven. Top with tomato slices and grated cheese. Bake 30 minutes longer. Serves 3 or 4.

Bing Crosby
Hollywood   January 7, 1953

Phyllis Condon
c/o D'Arcy Advertising Co.
515 Madison Avenue
New York, N. Y.

Dear Phyllis:

Thank you so much for your nice letter and for the pictures in color of that "cat" you are married to and my god-daughter. I must say my god-daughter looks very cute, but the king of the Gibson can't stand too much of a close-up. Neither can any of us as far as that goes.

May the new year for the Condon's be a happy and prosperous one, with crowds of clamorous jazz officianadoes beating at the doors of Mr. Condon's boite.

As ever,

Your friend,

Bing
Bing Crosby

BC:mj

oficinados

Searching for a sponsor: Christmas, Monmouth Beach, 1954

The old time wish—still ringing clear
Above the tumult and the fear
Among the sounds that underscore
The awesome jet-propellor's roar
The hi-fi blast—the freeway's hum
A wee, small voice for Christendom
"I wish you joy—I wish you love"
While snowflakes spell it out above
And angels sing it once again
The fondest hopes of gentle men
God rest you merry, lasses, lads
In private thoughts—in public ads
The traffic lights—still red and green
Help Santa, baby, make the scene
Distributing his gifts and toys
To all deserving girls and boys
The sleigh is faster than the truck
The doe is faster than the buck
So lay hypocrisy aside
This blessed, joyous Christmastide
And send the old time wish and prayer
To everybody, everywhere.
Lo! Two-score years ago—or so
I listed everyone I know
And tried to write a line or two
Incorporating all of you
But if I tried that feat this year
On every page there'd be a tear
So many gone—so many lost
—too often those we love the most—

My eye grows dim—my heart despairs
To think of all the empty chairs
So I just say to you—en masse,
Above the overflowing glass,
God bless you—each and every one
God bless your daughter—and your son
I send my friends, from A to Z
A kiss beneath their christmas tree
I'd list you singly, but, I mean,
I ain't no IBM machine!
I say the wish you may recall;
"A MERRY CHRISTMAS TO YOU ALL"
I write you joy, and peace, and cheer
And hope to see you all this year
We've been through wars, depressions, school
I'd say we've been around the pool
So I feel I've a right to say
A happy, holy Christmas day
And add this—from your humble versers
"A HAPPY NEW YEAR too!"

The Mercers

a special wish to all of You
— and Mezz & Ginny join me too!

TOO OLD TO TUNE UP...
1905 – 1944

Paul Smith is an art director whose hobby is guitar. He has the right idea. One day after work we were having a few drinks in a nearby bar and he casually asked me what I planned to do when I was forty. I said that by that time I'd be too old to tune up. Consequently the sketch he presented to me on my fortieth birthday.

Pee Wee and More Friends

Pee Wee Russell was born in St. Louis, Missouri, in 1906, and about the same time the earthquake in San Francisco occurred. It's still conjectural as to which one started shaking first. I think it was Pee Wee. He certainly has shaken some music out of his clarinet.

It is tough to write a description about Pee Wee. In the first place he was harmless. Even his dog Winkie was not scared of him. One day I ran into him on the street with Winkie. "How's Winkie?" I asked. "Eddie, Winkie is my heart," Pee Wee said. I don't know what Mary, Pee Wee's wife, said about this.

Aside from the clarinet, Pee Wee's personality was equally distinctive. He was not a ruffian at heart, but occasionally he might give you a dirty look if you forgot your manners. He never lost his. I remember one story that sums up his gentlemanly and gentle behavior. A wine-buyer came into Nick's one night and started spraying money like confetti. "Come on fellow," he'd say after every set, "and join me in a few quintuples." He wasn't obstreperous or even loud-mouthed, but he certainly was a hell of a customer. All night long we were knee-deep in his champagne. This fellow liked the whole band but Pee Wee was his special gem. After that first night, with all the money and champagne and all, the guy came back the next night. The above description still applies. We all joined him from force of habit. He put his arm around Pee Wee and said, "Well Pee Wee, how are you? How do you feel tonight? What do you say?" Pee Wee looked at him and said, "Long time no see."

PEE WEE IN THE EARLY TWENTIES WITH THE HERBERT BERGER
ORCHESTRA IN ST. LOUIS

*Pee Wee, about ready to drink his
empty wallet*

Tight like that. One way to earn money.

Pee Wee claimed this was his favorite picture. Max in the background, at the Ken Club in 1940.

Premoustache

Jam session, with Ernie Anderson

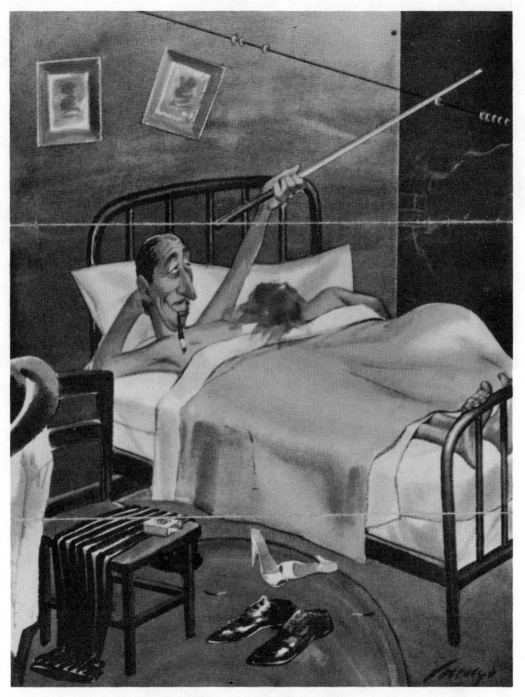

The artist didn't know Pee Wee. He didn't have to.

PEE WEE BY GEORGE WETTLING

Pee Wee wore out in the early fifties and no one expected he would recover. This picture by Genevieve Naylor captures a very worn out Pee Wee.

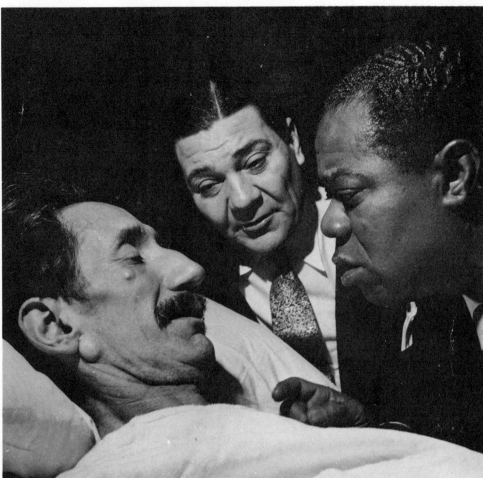

Pee Wee in the hospital in San Francisco with Jack Teagarden and Louis Armstrong

A BENEFIT IN CHICAGO

ZUTTY SINGLETON AND MARSHALL BROWN   LEE WILEY AND BOBBY HACKETT

YANK LAWSON AND JIMMY MC GRAW   JIMMY MC PARTLAND AND VERNON BROWN

Pee Wee made it in 1951. He didn't do so well in 1969. Five views of friends who came to pay tribute.

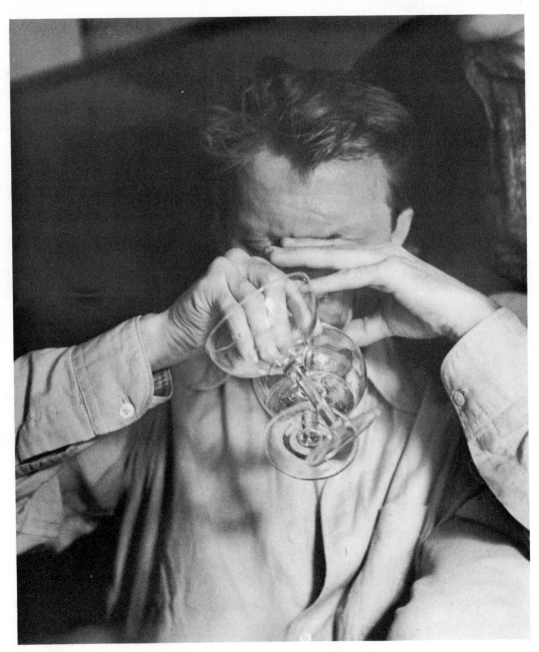

Never touch the stuff

On the sundeck at Monmouth Beach or in the kitchen, Johnny Mercer can relax at our house. Chemistry class in the kitchen.

(Above) Manassas, Virginia, 1970. A closeup of the Andrews Brothers.

(Right) Wild Bill in drag

Zutty leading a small but determined group

My daughter Maggie took this picture of Dick Wellstood just after he finished a solo record date. He couldn't have been happier.

Louis, Max, and Red at the short-lived Bourbon Street on Forty-Eighth Street. It looks as though they are watching the club close.

Jackie Gleason Midnight Special

DON EWELL, JERRY FULLER, MAX KAMINSKY, JACK TEAGARDEN

Rocking Chair

Between sets at the Riverboat. Bud Freeman and Clancy Hayes relax with Squirrel Ashcraft during the first run of the World's Greatest Jazz Band in New York City.

JACK BLAND, MEZZ, MAX, KANSAS FIELDS, GEORGE LUGG

Scarsdale High School in the late forties. This was a concert for a bunch of kids like Bob Wilber and Dick Wellstood. Now I'm happy when they will work with me.

Cutty Cutshall, Toronto, 1970. The next day Cutty didn't come down to the stand on time and he was a guy who was never late. He had died in his sleep. This is probably the last picture ever taken of him.

The last mile. Buzzy looks like he is on his way to the electric chair.

Kaiser Wilhelm and the Sauerkraut Six

George and Wingy Manone

DICK CARY

PEANUTS HUCKO, YANK LAWSON, AND BUZZY

With Hoagy Carmichael at a Sons of Indiana celebration

ZUTTY SINGLETON, JACK LESBERG, AND MAXINE SULLIVAN AT
MISHA REZNIKOFF'S

CHARLIE PETERSON, MANASSAS, VIRGINIA, 1970

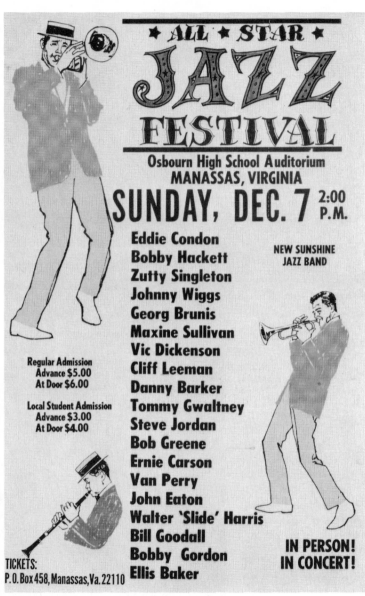

★ ALL ★ STAR ★
JAZZ
FESTIVAL
Osbourn High School Auditorium
MANASSAS, VIRGINIA
SUNDAY, DEC. 7 2:00 P.M.

Eddie Condon
Bobby Hackett
Zutty Singleton
Johnny Wiggs
Georg Brunis
Maxine Sullivan
Vic Dickenson
Cliff Leeman
Danny Barker
Tommy Gwaltney
Steve Jordan
Bob Greene
Ernie Carson
Van Perry
John Eaton
Walter 'Slide' Harris
Bill Goodall
Bobby Gordon
Ellis Baker

NEW SUNSHINE
JAZZ BAND

Regular Admission
Advance $5.00
At Door $6.00

Local Student Admission
Advance $3.00
At Door $4.00

IN PERSON!
IN CONCERT!

TICKETS:
P.O. Box 458, Manassas, Va. 22110

PUG HORTON AND DILL JONES AT THE MANASSAS JAZZ FESTIVAL

Shall I lead the ensemble?

ZUTTY AND MARGE SINGLETON. JOHN EATON
IN BACKGROUND.

Stern leadership

TONY PARENTI AND JOHN EATON

LOU MCGARITY

Nick's has turned into a place called Your Father's Moustache. It is disheartening but some of my friends play at the jam sessions on Sunday night: Lou McGarity, Ed Polcer, and Ken Davern.

Louis in later years, with Joe Muranyi

Joe Venuti playing better than ever at Sherman Fairchild's

There are still private parties on Long Island. Joe Muranyi, George, Vic, Danny Barker, and Johnny Windhurst made this one.

TAKE TEA AND SEE

Concerts and Tours

I played in my first jazz concert in 1936. Thirty-six years later I was still in the concert halls at Carnegie Hall in New York City during the 1972 Newport Jazz Festival. There have been many in between that took me to some interesting places in the United States and various parts of the world.

Program

RED NORVO AND HIS SWINGTETTE
with Mildred Bailey, Guest Star

Bass	Peter Peterson
Drums	Maurice Purtill
Tenor Sax	Herbert Haymer
Cornet	Stu Fletcher
Clarinet	Slats Long
Guitar	Dave Barber
Xylophone	Red Norvo

Courtesy of Music Corp. of America, Hotel Commodore

**STUFF SMITH AND
HIS ONYX CLUB BAND**

Stuff Smith	Violin
Jonah Jones	Trumpet
Cozy Cole	Drums
Raymond Smith	Piano
Robert Bennett	Guitar
Mac Walker	Bass
Baby White	Vocalist

Courtesy of Consolidated Radio Artists, Inc.

BUNNY BERRIGAN AND HIS SWING GANG

Bunny Berrigan	Trumpet
Eddie Condon	Guitar
Forrest Crawford	Tenor Saxophone
Marty Stulmaker	Bass
Joe Bushkin	Piano
Sam Weiss	Drums

Courtesy of "18" Club

CASPER REARDON
Radio's Outstanding Swing Harpist

TOMMY DORSEY AND HIS CLAMBAKE "7"

Tenor Sax	Bud Freeman
Clarinet	Joe Dixon
Trumpet	Max Kamensky
Trombone	Tommy Dorsey
Drums	Davey Tough
Guitar	Carmen Mastren
Bass	Gene Trexler
Piano	Dick Jones
Vocalist	Edythe Wright

Courtesy of Music Corp. of America and Hotel Lincoln

Intermission 15 minutes

My first appearance at a jazz concert, just out of the hospital in 1936. Joe Helbock of the Onyx Club sponsored it.

JAZZ PLAYERS BARRED—Eddie Condon, seated on the steps of Constitution Hall yesterday with his guitar, which the DAR says will never be heard in the Eighteenth street house.
—Star Staff Photo.

Man With 1000 Fingers Points 'Em All at DAR

In answer to a husky voice on the telephone late yesterday afternoon, I dropped down to the Willard Hotel to have a chat with Eddie Condon, most recent victim of the D. A. R.'s inflexible ideas as to whom shall be entertained in Constitution Hall and by whom. Condon had no fears on the race question when he applied for the D. A. R.'s hallowed hall, but they answered that the type of audience accustomed to attending his concerts might become too enthusiastic and wreck the joint.

Not even a $100,000 surety bond or the fact that Condon's aggregations have been playing for years in New York's Carnegie Hall or Boston's Symphony Hall could sway them. To the D. A. R., hep cats are undesirable—and that's that.

Anyway, Eddie was down, after a bollixed-up plane trip from New York that left him even more sleepy-eyed than ever, making arrangements for a place to play. He and his manager settled on the Willard Hotel ballroom, which they booked for March 25. He's bringing an aggregation with him that will make you listeners to late music from the night club stare at the list with disbelief. Here it is: piano, Joe Sullivan, Gene Schroeder and Joe Bushkin; cornet, Wild Bill Davison; trumpet, Muggsy Spanier; clarinet, Tony Parenti, Peewee Russell and Joe Dixon; trombone, George Brunis and Brad Gowans; bass, Jack Leeburg, and drum, George Wetling.

Condon Needles DAR For Constitution Hall Ban in D.C. Concert

Washington, March 26.

If any Daughters of the American Revolution sneaked into the Willard ballroom last night (25) to hear Eddie Condon and his jazz men they are probably wishing they had given him the use of Constitution Hall. The 15 musicians who gave Washington jazz fans a concert of the righteous stuff also improvised dozens of gags about the DAR. Both the music and the gags sent the 600 or so hepsters who shelled out $3.60 each into ecstasies.

Max Kaminsky played a special "DAR Blues." When the spot got in Condon's eyes, he muttered something about "A DAR Aiming That Thing at Me," and in the only serious moment of the evening, the emcee pointed out that the leader's father is a member of the Sons of the American Revolution and that his two daughters are eligible to join the DAR.

DAR nixed Condon's use of its hall for the concert on the ground that jazz was too undignified for the place.

Condon Band Barred At Constitution Hall

Denied use of Constitution Hall for a jazz concert by the Daughters of the American Revolution because his orchestra plays the type of music which might attract less desirable elements of the population, Eddie Condon, the New York "Swing King" came here yesterday to complete a deal to play in the Willard Hotel ballroom March 25 instead.

The little man with the bow tie bristled with indignation when questioned about the controversy which resulted in the DAR ban against appearance of his jazz band in Constitution Hall.

"They oughtn't of done it," he said.

Asked to comment on reasons for denying use of the hall, Fred Hand, manager, declared: "We refuse to give any statement at all."

After a success or two in concert halls someone said I should take a band into Washington, D.C. We were set to play Constitution Hall, which is owned by the DAR. At the last moment we were informed by the daughters of the awful right that we could not play in their hall because we used "mixed" bands and might draw "undesirable" elements. I was locked out and decided to let everybody know it. This picture ran on the front page of the Washington Post and Time did a story as well. We didn't need the publicity because we had already shifted the concert to the Willard Hotel and we jammed the place. The Willard is abandoned now and I think demolished. The DAR probably blames that on us.

One of our tours took us as far west as Minneapolis. Dmitri Mitropoulos led the orchestra there and he stopped in to say hello. He liked jazz.

In 1954 a man named Ralph Black contacted me and asked if I would like to take a band to Buffalo to play with the town's local string band, the Buffalo Philharmonic. I had played in some pretty fancy halls in the past but I was usually in charge and this was to be a different kind of mixed band. I was afraid the fruit might fly. The dowagers would be expecting Beethoven's fifth and would wind up with Condon's quart.

The leader of the Buffalo band was a bass player named Willis Page and we got together before the concert and posed for this dueling picture, with Hackett and Lesberg encouraging. There was no need for a duel: the concert was a success, with about three thousand screaming people in the audience. When Page joined my band on a borrowed string bass for the final number, the great acoustics in Kleinhan's Hall could barely stand it.

We made a little history that night. It was the first time a jazz band and a symphony had ever played together. Lots of people have tried it since and some people have even gone so far as scoring music for the affairs, but on that August night in 1954 we gave the first dual concert of its kind.

In 1955 Black got after me again and asked if I would like to follow up my Buffalo success with an adventure in Washington, D.C. I signed on for two concerts with the National Symphony in January 1956 and then I found out that one of the concerts was to be held in Constitution Hall. I had been banned from the place only a few years before, but everything worked out fine this time. Phyllis, Maggie, Liza, and Squirrel Ashcraft all sat watching from the Presidential Box and there were no immediate disasters.

The big band played Mozart, Strauss, and Beethoven. We played Armstrong and Impromptu Ensemble. The hall was sold out and was full of black, white, yellow, and brown people, all sitting side by side. Nobody walked out and the affair was one of my happiest moments. Howard Mitchell, the Music Director of the orchestra, said it was a privilege to have me and that my music caused a lot of people to go to Constitution Hall that ordinarily would not be there. I told him I was one of these people.

MUSIC

Topnotch *Tannhäuser*

One conductor slammed down his baton, grumbled *"auf Wiedersehen,"* and walked out. Leading singers caught colds in the wet July weather. Technicians scrambled to lighten the murky stage so that the audience could see more of what was going on. After six weeks of preparing the season, Wieland and Wolfgang Wagner last week raised the curtain on the opening production, their grandfather's *Tannhäuser*. Despite all crises, the production turned out topnotch.

Bayreuth had not dared do *Tannhäuser* since Toscanini's unforgettable version 24 years ago. But brothers Wieland and Wolfgang, who will dare anything, decided the old Venusberg needed some drastic new landscaping. They hired fast-rising, Kiev-born Conductor Igor Markevitch, who had never done Wagnerian opera before, then replaced him with Germany's Joseph Keilberth. "I was not aware that anybody here was interested in tempo," huffed Markevitch at one point. "All they talk about is lighting"—and no wonder, for Director Wieland Wagner's new staging relies mainly on light effects. When the trumpets announced curtain time one afternoon last week, nobody at Bayreuth quite knew what to expect.

Musically, the production proved to be more than adequate, despite the fact that Tenor Ramon Vinay and pretty Soprano Gre Brouenstein showed signs of strain. The chorus, one of the world's finest, performed brilliantly. But the chief attraction, as usual, was the staging. Wieland sees *Tannhäuser* as a harried misfit in a world of rigid conventions. Dressed in a black cloak (while the other minstrels wear brown), he moves among stiff, almost mechanized people of the court. Preparing for the crucial song contest in the second act—usually staged with casual confusion—uniformly dressed men and women march into the hall in stiff military style. But the orgiastic Venusberg scene, set in flowing concentric circles of light, is heavily sensual: the ballet flings itself into bumps and grinds that rival the old Minsky's.

After the final curtain, half of the Bayreuth audience seemed in tears, clapped for 15 minutes. With *Tannhäuser*, the Bayreuth brothers have now redraped all the standard Wagner works in their new, bare, dramatically lighted dress. Their style has become a prototype for new Wagner productions in most major opera houses. Notable exception: New York's Metropolitan, whose Wagner producers seem never to have heard of Bayreuth's lighting, let alone Minsky's.

Cats by the Sea

At Newport, the weathering old mansions of the rich still brood by the sea, and outsiders half expect to meet ladies in ankle-dusting tennis skirts escorted by blades in gaily banded boaters. But last week Newport's narrow streets were thronged with loud-shirted bookie types from Broadway, young intellectuals in need of haircuts, crew-cut Ivy Leaguers, sailors, Harlem girls with extravagant hairdos and high-school girls in shorts. They were cats. From as far away as Kansas they had come to hear a two-day monster jazz festival.

The Newport wingding was further evidence that jazz is enjoying its biggest boom in years, with record sales soaring and nightclubs sprouting new jazz acts all over the country. A crowd of 6,000 fans jammed into Newport's dingy old open-air Casino for the first-night concert. There was a clear moon overhead as Old-

NEWPORT JAM SESSION*
From a crooked trumpet, a pounding of bricks.

timer Eddie Condon, a little ill at ease in all the fresh air, stamped his foot four times and swung into *Muskrat Ramble*, sweeping along his bang-up Dixieland outfit, including Clarinetist Pee Wee Russell, Trumpeter Wild Bill Davison, Pianist Ralph Sutton. The music was hot, and the crowd warmed to it with shouts of "Go! Go!"

Up to the Stars. From the oldtime start, the music came gradually up to date. Things really began to hum when Bop Trumpeter Dizzy Gillespie took the stage with his quintet. Looking bemused and gesturing wildly, he set his cocked trumpet* to his lips and played Gabriel-like tones that sent chills up the listeners' spines. "See, that's a square bend," he explained, pointing to the upswept angle. "Well, I get a sort of square note out of there. When you say 'Pow-w-w,' it comes out like a pounding—like a pounding of bricks."

When Pianist Oscar Peterson and his

---

* Specially constructed with its bell tilted upward at a 45-degree angle. Dizzy discovered the new twist after a party accident bent his horn. When he played it, he was amazed: "For the first time I heard myself play."

trio gave a fast-fingered version of *Tenderly* sprinkled with suave dissonances, the modernist crowd was ready to call it the high point of the festival. But the younger set shrieked louder when hollow-cheeked Gerry Mulligan bellowed and coaxed *The Lady Is a Tramp* through his big baritone sax. The concert finally ended after midnight with a 20-man jam session that sent the strangest sounds ever heard in Newport floating up to the stars.

In the Black. Next night there was another big concert in the Casino with a few other name combos (*e.g.*, Pianists George Shearing, Erroll Garner, Lennie Tristano) plus informal sessions that lasted till dawn. In the afternoon a slim crowd of cats had attended a forum about the origin and meaning of jazz. But the meaning of the festival itself seemed to be that jazz—whether Dixieland, bop or "modern"—more than ever has America's ear. The festival wound up tidily in the black.

Tired of Listening

Being a music critic and a composer at the same time is a little like playing quarterback and simultaneously having to blow the referee's whistle. But Composer-Critic Virgil Thomson has long managed to write his own music and blow the whistle on the music of others without missing a play. Whether he was reporting on the nuances in a symphony performance, "discovering" a debutante performer, delivering an essay on one of the intricacies of composition itself, or unabashedly plugging his own works, he hardly ever bored a reader. Last week, after 14 years of what he calls a "honeymoon" with New York's *Herald Tribune*, waspish Virgil Thomson, 57, announced that he was "tired of listening to music," was quitting to do more composing, lecturing and conducting.

Musician by inclination and wit by

---

* From left: Jazzmen Russell, Mulligan, Condon,

NEWPORT JAM SESSION

The first Newport Jazz Festival was in 1954 and someone asked me to participate. A few thousand dowagers and psychiatrists attended, as did every jazz musician on the East Coast. We played outside for the concert and I was ill at ease in the fresh air but I managed. At the concert the next year we had to play in a driving rainstorm. It was recorded and was my first underwater recording.

Baltimore Symphony Orchestra

PETER HERMAN ADLER, Music Director and Conductor

120 WEST MT. ROYAL AVENUE · BALTIMORE 1, MD.

TELEPHONE SARATOGA 7-7300

RALPH BLACK
MANAGER

23
January
1963

Mr. Eddie Condon
27 Washington Square, North
New York 11, New York

Dear Eddie:

The performance Saturday will be at 8:30 p.m. The rehearsal
will be at 2:30 p.m. Perhaps you would want to come down and
listen to the rehearsal, because, after all, you are going to
have to jazz up a few of the serious melodies which we are
playing.

The works which you are going to have to play are as follows:

Stranger in Paradise (Polovtzian Dances by Borodin)
Moon Love (Symphony No. 5, 2nd Movement, Tschaikovsky)
Blue Danube in jazz time
Carmen: Toreador Song, Habanera, Sequidille

In addition to this, you will have two sets of your own and these
will be about 12 minutes each. You can make up your own list
here, but for heaven's sake include Muscrat Ramble and When the
Saints Go Marching In. I presume that you will follow the usual
course and announce these as you go along.

Is there anybody in your group who could do anything with the
symphony which would make sense? You will recall that Bobby
Hackett played Funny Valentine with the symphony in Washington and
it was a big hit. If you have anybody and the arrangements to go
with it, we would like this type of thing. In any case, we will
want to conclude the jazz portion with a member of our orchestra
sitting in with you for a couple of choruses. His name is John
Melick, our principal trombone, and he has played with Benny Goodman
and all the big bands.

Don't forget that this will be broadcast in stereo. It won't make
any difference, except perhaps in your comments. Let me know if

---

Mr. Eddie Condon
23 January 1963
Page Two

you can make the rehearsal, as we should go over some programs
before the concert. You could take the 11 a.m. train out of
New York which arrives here at 2:08. There is a train which
leaves Baltimore to New York at 11:01 p.m. You could make it
in plenty of time, as the hall is only three blocks from the
railroad station.

Kindest regards,

Ralph Black

BALTIMORE SYMPHONY ORCHESTRA

FIFTH SATURDAY EVENING CONCERT

JANUARY 26, 1963 — 8:30 P. M.

ELYAKUM SHAPIRA, Conducting

EDDIE CONDON AND HIS ALL STARS
Buck Clayton, Peanuts Hucko, Lou McGarrity
Johnny Varro, Jack Lesberg

**The entire Saturday Evening Pops Concerts Series is sponsored by
The National Brewing Company**

JAZZ VS CLASSICS

PROGRAM

BALTIMORE SYMPHONY: Polovtzian Dances from "Prince Igor"....Borodin
EDDIE CONDON AND HIS ALL STARS: Stranger in Paradise

BALTIMORE SYMPHONY:
  Symphony #5 (second movement) Andante Cantabile...Tchaikovsky
EDDIE CONDON AND HIS ALL STARS: Moon Love

DIXIELAND GROUP BY MR. CONDON

BALTIMORE SYMPHONY: El Salon Mexico.....................Copland

INTERMISSION

*The entire Saturday Evening Pop Concert Series is sponsored by the
National Brewing Company and broadcast in stereo over WBAL
AM and FM.
Musical portions of the broadcasts of the Baltimore Symphony
Orchestra are under the technical supervision of Recordings Incor-
porated of Baltimore.*

BALTIMORE SYMPHONY: Espana ....Chabrier

BALTIMORE SYMPHONY: Blue Danube Waltz...................Strauss
EDDIE CONDON AND HIS ALL STARS: Swinging the Blues on the Danube

GROUP BY MR. CONDON AND HIS ALL STARS

EDDIE CONDON AND HIS ALL STARS: Carmen in Ragtime
BALTIMORE SYMPHONY: Suite from "Carmen".....................Bizet

    I.   Aragondaise
   II. Seguedille
  III. Les Dragons D'Alcala
  IV. Habanera
   V. Les Toreadors

*THE BALTIMORE SYMPHONY USES THE BALDWIN PIANO COURTESY OF
THE KUNKEL PIANO COMPANY*

NOTICE: For your own safety, LOOK for your nearest EXIT.
In case of emergency WALK, do not RUN, to that EXIT.
By order of the Mayor and City Council of Baltimore

---

*Ralph was still at it in 1963. We moved up to Balti-
more. This will give you an idea what the real big bands
think about.*

In 1956 I took a group to England: Wild Bill, Cutty, Bob Wilber, Gene Schroeder, Leonard Gaskin, and George Wettling. I knew we were welcome the minute we arrived because there were four bands to greet us at the airport. The combined sounds of Humphrey Littleton, Chris Barber, Mick Mulligan, and Beryl Bryden drowned out the sound of the airplanes. These guys played what they called "traditional" jazz; we sounded modern by comparison.

Every time one of the guys in the band took a drink there was a reporter to cover it and usually the papers ran stories that none of us ever drew a sober breath the entire time we were in the country. Wild Bill started off by trying to steal Big Ben but the chimes scared him away. George Wettling purposely came over with light wearing apparel, having planned in front to buy up as many Scotch and English clothes as possible. He bought so many that Cutty remarked that George had even bought tweed underwear. Bob Wilber and Leonard Gaskins were the youngest members of the band, but I rarely saw them except on stage; they were running around collecting souvenirs and sightseeing.

Our first concert was in Glasgow and we got off to a rocky start but by the end of the night we brought down the roof, particularly when Humphrey Littleton's band joined us on stage. The tour was off to a good start and from then on we played just like it was Third Street and we hit most of the major cities in England.

STOLL THEATER CONCERT

PUB CRAWLING AFTER THE CONCERT

WITH HUMPHREY LITTLETON ON STAGE

Hello Central, give me Doctor Jazz

George Wettling took this photo outside the Golden Fleece Inn.

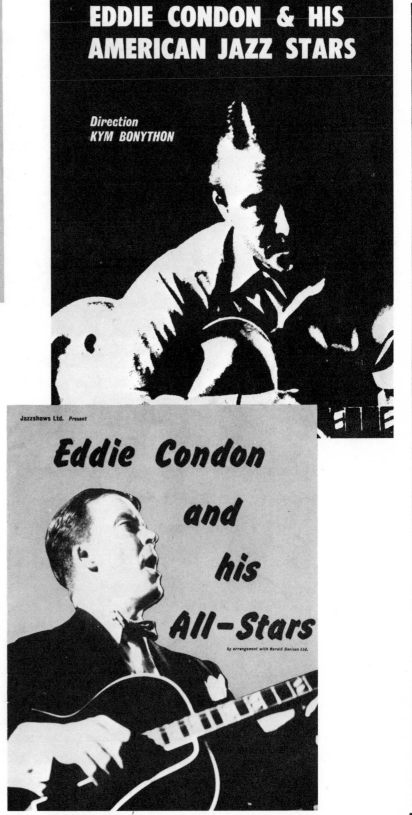

NEW ZEALAND MUSICIANS' UNION
(AUCKLAND BRANCH)

We are proud to extend

Honorary Membership

To *EDDIE CONDON*

A VISITOR

From *United States, America*

President *Norris H. Cooper.* Secretary *Thos. E. Skinner.*

Date *16th March 1964*

EDDIE CONDON & HIS
AMERICAN JAZZ STARS

Direction
KYM BONYTHON

EDDIE CONDON
AND HIS ALL STARS

PRESENTED BY THE NEW ZEALAND BROADCASTING CORPORATION

Jazzshows Ltd. Present

Eddie Condon
and
his
All-Stars

by arrangement with Harold Davison Ltd.

In 1964 I took a band to Japan, Australia, and New Zealand. We made it back.

Pee Wee and I at Billy Banks' club in Tokyo, 1964

Jimmy Rushing and I in Australia

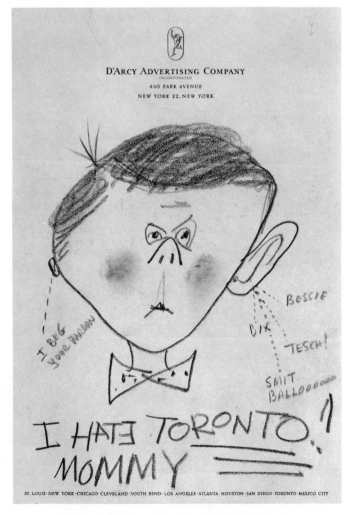

Inaugural Ball Chart

Location	Master of Ceremonies	Bands & Combos	Cabinet & VIPs		States	
SHOREHAM	Lee Bowman	Doc Severinsen Bob Cross Eddie Condon Tiny Meeker	Melvin R. Laird, Secy. Defense Winton M. Blount, Postmaster General	Kansas Maine New Mexico North Dakota	Ohio Puerto Rico South Carolina Wisconsin	

In 1969 I played my first Inaugural Ball. Bill Hearst as a personal favor set it up for me and I took a good band to Washington. We played the Shoreham and had a good time before and after the ball.

Boss — Youre letter was a surprise — a pleasant one — dont lose my address — playing the bleached house would be my all time valentine —

Eddie Condon

The President wrote me a thank-you letter and invited me to play a party at the White House. My answer.

ALICE TULLY HALL
LINCOLN CENTER FOR THE PERFORMING ARTS

Thursday Evening, September 30, 1971, at 8:30

STARS OF JAZZ

EDDIE CONDON, Guitar **ART HODES**, Piano **BARNEY BIGARD**, Clarinet
WILD BILL DAVISON, Trumpet **ROBERT "RAIL" WILSON**, Bass
JIM BEEBE, Trombone **HILLARD BROWN**, Drums

Introduction . . . It all began with a beat . . . Drums

Just a Closer Walk with You
(A SPIRITUAL)

MELROSE - NEW ORLEANS RHYTHM KINGS	Tin Roof Blues (A BLUES)
PORTER STEELE - W. MELROSE	High Society (NEW ORLEANS PARADE STYLE MUSIC)
PRIMROSE	Saint James Infirmary (A DIRGE)
ORY - GILBERT	Muskrat Ramble (NEW ORLEANS JAZZ STYLE)
"JELLY ROLL" MORTON	Grandpa's Spells (RAGTIME)
TRADITIONAL	When the Saints Go Marching In (A JOYFUL SOUND)

INTERMISSION

THE CHICAGO PERIOD

LA ROCCA - SHIELDS	At the Jazz Band Ball (REMEMBERING BIX BEIDERBECKE)
	Blue Again (IN APPRECIATION OF LOUIS ARMSTRONG)
BROOKS	Darktown Strutters Ball (CHICAGO, THAT TODDLIN' TOWN)
CLIFF BURWELL - MITCHEL PARISH	Sweet Lorraine (THE BALLAD WITH FEELING)
DURANTE - BARNETT	Bill Bailey (GOOD-TIME JAZZ)

BLUES AND JAZZ

	Hey, Mr. Piano Man, Give Us a Tune (THE PIANO STYLES OF THE PIANO GREATS OF YESTERYEAR: JIMMY YANCEY, PINE TOP SMITH, JAMES P. JOHNSON, FATS WALLER. THE RHYTHM SECTION JOINS IN)
IMPROVISED	Remembering Kansas City (SOUL MUSIC)
BERNIE-PINKARD-CASEY	Sweet Georgia Brown (RHYTHM IS OUR BUSINESS)
J. PETTIS - B. MEYERS - E. SCHOEBEL	Bugle Call Rag (REMINISCENT OF THE SUNDAY-AFTERNOON JAM SESSIONS ON 52ND STREET)

COLUMBIA ARTISTS THEATRICALS CORP.
Personal Direction: CHARLES K. JONES
165 West 57th Street, New York, New York 10019

The taking of photographs and the use of recording equipment are not allowed in this auditorium. Members of the audience who must leave the auditorium before the end of the concert are earnestly requested to do so between numbers, not during the performance.

THE ALICE TULLY HALL PROGRAM, published by Saturday Review, Inc., 380 Madison Avenue, New York, N.Y. 10017. STAFF FOR THE ALICE TULLY HALL PROGRAM: William D. Patterson, Publisher; Herbert J. Teison, Associate Publisher; Richard L. Tobin, Associate Publisher; Irving Kolodin, Editorial Director; Norman Cousins, Chairman of the Editorial Board; Roanne Alpert, Managing Editor; Irving Spellens, Art Director; Joseph Gasparino, Production Manager.

On tour Fall, 1971. Columbia Artists put together a seven-week tour for some of us who were still alive. After it was over we looked back and saw that we had been shuffled through twenty-six states. We were sold out for almost every concert and the audiences were enthusiastic.

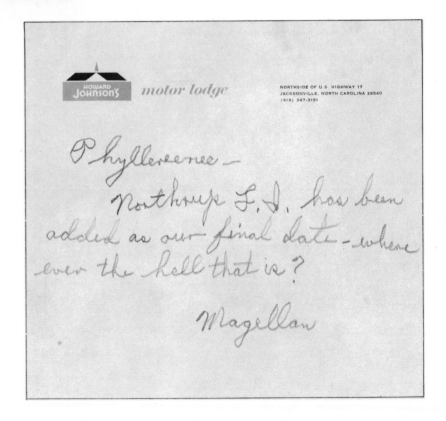

Phyllereenee —

Northrup L. I. has been added as our final date — where ever the hell that is?

Magellan

Carnegie Hall—1972
(courtesy Jeff Atterton)